Official Cambridge Exam Preparation

Kid's Box
New Generation

British English

Caroline Nixon &
Michael Tomlinson

CAMBRIDGE

Pupil's Book 6
with eBook

Language summary

Smart technology

What technology do you use at home?

1 ▶ **What's the competition? Watch and check.**

2 ▶ **Watch again and number the sentences.**

1 We can go to your house after that. ☐
2 Hi, Meera. How are you? 1
3 We can write the best blog in the country. ☐
4 There's a new blog competition online. ☐
5 I've got a message from Meera. ☐

STUDY

Where **is** he?
The children **have to** change their books.
The winners **can** enter the international blog competition.
Stella **thinks** it sounds exciting.

3 **Read and choose the right words.**

1 Lenny **doesn't** / **don't** arrive early.
2 Where **has** / **is** Lenny?
3 Stella and Lenny **have** / **has** to change their books at the library.
4 Lenny **is** / **has** got a message from Meera.
5 There **are** / **is** a prize for the best blog.
6 The winners can **enter** / **entering** the international blog competition next year.
7 Why **don't** / **doesn't** we do our first blog post on technology?
8 Stella thinks it **sound** / **sounds** exciting.

4 **Ask and answer.**

1 What's the prize for the competition? Why do they want to win it?
2 Have you ever entered a big competition? What did you do?

1 Can you remember the last lesson? Watch the language video.

2 Read. Then listen and say 'yes' or 'no'. Correct the wrong sentences.

National Blog Competition

Write a blog and help your school. It's open to all schools with students between the ages of 7 and 12. Students must write a blog post every month. The blog post should be interesting and include text and photos.

There are two important prizes. The best blog wins **new tablets** for everyone in your class. The winners can also enter the international blog competition next year.

3 Read and answer.

Stella: Hi everyone. So … let's talk about our first blog post for the competition.

Meera: Yes, great. What kind of technology should we write about?

Lenny: Why don't we write about video games?

Meera: Good idea, Lenny!

Stella: Yes, I like that suggestion, but we should also write about other things. I'd like to write about online learning.

Lenny: OK. Shall I write about video games? Then you can write about online learning, Stella. What do you think, Meera?

Meera: That sounds good to me. Maybe I can write about technology at home?

Stella: Yes, I love that idea. OK everyone, no more chatting! Let's do it!

Lenny: See you at school tomorrow!

1 What are they chatting about?
2 What would Lenny like to write about?
3 Does Meera like Lenny's suggestion?
4 What does Stella think they should do?
5 Does Stella want to write about online shopping?
6 What's Meera going to write about?
7 Who wants to start now?
8 When are they going to meet again?

4 Imagine you're going to write a blog post about school. In groups, ask and answer.

1 What do you want to write about? Why?
2 Do your friends want to write about the same thing? Why or why not?

Useful language

Let's (talk about) …
What about …?
Why don't we (write about) …?
That sounds good to me.
Good idea.
I like that idea/suggestion, but we should …

5 Write your blog post: My school. Write 30–40 words.

1 Read the blog. What can technology give us? Find five things.

ALL BLOGS | MY BLOG | NEW POST

Kid's Box Reports

Technology is changing our lives a lot, so this is the topic of our first blog post. People use technology every day when they work, study or play.

Technology

We all use electronic devices like PCs (personal computers), **laptops**, **tablets** and **smartphones** to connect with people and programmes **online**. These days most people have **Wi-Fi** at home, and we use different programmes and apps to go online.

Online learning

In some parts of the world children don't go to school. They learn in an online classroom where they can communicate with their teachers and friends. Students have to turn on their cameras so that the teacher and class can see them, and the computer **screen** becomes their classroom and whiteboard. They use **headphones** or speakers to listen, and they talk into a **microphone**. When they have to do homework, they can send their teacher a **file** by **email** or they can **upload** it in an **app**.

Video games

Playing **video games** is one of the biggest hobbies for young people today. People can connect with lots of players in different places all over the world to play and **chat** online.

E-sports is a kind of **competition** using video games for teams or single players. Millions of people can watch the competitors playing online and it's very exciting. For some people, it is their job to play in online competitions and they can earn money. We call these people gamers.

Technology at home

These days a lot of homes have a **smart speaker**. This can answer questions about the weather, music or TV programmes and, using Wi-Fi, people can connect it to other devices and ask it to do things. It can make a shopping list, **turn** the TV **on** or **off**, or control the temperature at home. Technology also helps in other ways. People can connect cameras in their house or garden, and watch their pets! Then, when they are not at home, they can watch what their pets are doing and make sure they're safe.

2 Read again and correct the sentences.

1 Laptops, tablets and plants are electronic devices.
2 In an online classroom, students can communicate with teachers and insects.
3 When they have to do homework, they can send their teacher a postcard by email.
4 E-sports is a kind of meal using video games.
5 People can watch online competitions and it's very boring.
6 People can't earn money by playing in video game competitions.
7 Smart speakers can make the beds.
8 With microphones people can see the inside of their houses on their screens.

3 Talk to your partner.

1 Which of these do you use at home?
2 What kind of technology would you like to have? Why?

I always send my homework to my teacher through our school app.

I would like to have a smart speaker at home because I want to ask it lots of questions.

1 Read and complete.

A smart speaker in the hall | And send photos to our friends | ~~Headphones and big touch screens~~ | Now turn off the Wi-Fi | We can use some apps as dictionaries

We've got tablets in our schoolbags,
An electronic smartboard on the wall.
There are laptops,
(1) Headphones and big touch screens.
Hear the future call!

We've got online learning,
We use smart technology
To find out what words mean,
(2) ______________________

Video things on our phones
(3) ______________________.
We chat on our video games
And use programs to connect.

(4) ______________________,
And go out in the street.
You love chatting with all your friends
Every time you meet.

There are robots in our homes now,
(5) ______________________.
It can answer everything we ask,
Hear the future call!

2 3–4 Listen and check. Then do karaoke.

3 Read and complete.

app | chat | ~~download~~ | file | internet | likes | online | screen

Lenny
Last week I got a cool new video game. The program was really big, so it took a long time to (1) download, but it's brilliant. On Saturday I'm going to play and (2) ________ online with friends from all over the world.

Meera
I enjoy taking photos and making videos. I share them (3) ________ with a great (4) ________ called CoolChat, which all of my friends use, too. I post my photos there and I sometimes get a lot of (5) ________ ♥.

Stella
I love connecting to the (6) ________ to get information for my homework. I use my tablet, which has got a touch (7) ________, so it's faster for me to work. I've finished my project on technology and I've saved it in a big (8) ________. This evening I'm going to upload it for my teacher to read.

4 Write about how you use technology. Write 30–40 words.

Sounds and life skills

Being a good school citizen

1 Watch the video. How do they feel after they read about the competition?

Pronunciation focus

2 5 Listen and underline the stress in the words in bold. Write the words.

MEERA: … let's write something for this **competition** and win those new **tablets** for our class.

LENNY: Why don't we do our first blog on **technology**?

STELLA: Great idea, Lenny! That sounds very **exciting**!

Oo	laptop keyboard ______
Ooo	internet microphone
oOo	computer ______
oOoo	______
ooOo	______

3 6 Listen and complete. Practise with a partner.

A: What technology do you use every day?
B: I use the ______ for my homework.

A: Have you got a ______, a ______ or a ______?
B: I've got a ______.

4 Look and write more ideas.

How to be a good school citizen

5 In pairs, make a poster about how to be a good school citizen.

Useful language

We can write …
We have to …
I think it's important to …

Diggory Bones

7

1 **What time's Diggory's talk? What does Diggory have to do to show the next photo?**

1 Beastly tales

What stories about animals do you know?

1 What's Stella good at? Watch and check.

2 Watch again and answer the questions.

1 What time's the audition going to be? *Quarter to four.*
2 Who's going to go to the audition?
3 Which part is she going to do in the audition?
4 Who's going to be King of the Beasts?
5 Which part are they going to give Stella?
6 Are they going to write about the school play?

3 Read and match.

1 Who's going to
2 The audition
3 Stella's going to
4 Meera and Lenny are
5 Stella isn't going
6 Meera and Lenny aren't going
7 What are they going

a is going to be on Wednesday.
b to be in the play.
c go to the audition.
d to be the monkey.
e to write about?
f be in the play?
g going to watch her.

STUDY

I'm **going to go** to the audition.
We **aren't going to choose** you.
Are you **going to be** in the play?
What's Stella **going to be** in the play?

4 Ask and answer.

1 What did you think of Stella's acting?
2 Do you like acting? Would you like to be in a school play?

Language: plans, intentions and predictions with *going to*

1 Can you remember the last lesson? Watch the language video.

2 Choose words from the box to complete the text.

bird cinema ~~going~~ have island pets restaurant rocks see want

Helen and Robert are (1) ___going___ to go to the (2) ______ tomorrow. They're going to (3) ______ a film called **My Family and Other Animals**. The film's from a book by Gerald Durrell and it's about his life when he was ten years old. In the film, the boy lives on an (4) ______. He's got some friends, but a lot of his friends are different (5) ______. He's got a (6) ______ called Ulysses, a tortoise called Achilles and lots of spiders. Helen and Robert are going to have a great time because it's a very funny film.

3 Read again and answer. Check with a partner.

1 Where are Helen and Robert going to go?
2 What are they going to see?
3 What's the film about?
4 How old is Gerald in the book?
5 What pets has Gerald got?
6 Why are Helen and Robert going to enjoy the film?

4 Read and cross out the extra word.

1 We're are going to go to the theatre tomorrow.
2 We aren't going to see at **The Lion King**.
3 I'm going to visit to my grandmother on Sunday.
4 What are you to going to see?
5 Where do are you going to sit?
6 She isn't going to sing on tonight.

5 Write questions with 'going to'.

1 Who / see / weekend?
2 What / do / Monday / after school?
3 play basketball / tomorrow afternoon?
4 Where / go / Friday / after school?
5 What / watch / TV / tomorrow?
6 When / do / your homework?

1 Who are you going to see at the weekend?

6 Ask and answer.

Who are you going to see at the weekend?

I'm going to see my cousins.

7 Write about what you're going to do next week. Write 30–40 words.

1 Read the blog. How many of the beasts are part bird?

ALL BLOGS | MY BLOG | NEW POST

Kid's Box Reports

There are many ancient stories from different countries. Some are about heroes and strange and exciting beasts which aren't real. These stories are called myths.

Myths

Griffins have got the head, wings, front legs and **claws** of an **eagle**, and the body and back legs of a lion. They make **nests** from gold.

A **unicorn** is a beautiful white horse with one long **horn** on its head. It's got a goat's feet and beard, and a lion's tail.

A **dragon** is a beast which has got the body of a lizard, so dragons haven't got **fur** like a cat or **feathers** like a bird; they've got **scales** like a fish. Some dragons have got wings like a bat, and some can **breathe** fire.

Sirens and **harpies** are both part bird, part woman, but they're different. Sirens live near water. They sing beautifully, but they're dangerous because people sail their boats onto rocks to listen to them. Harpies can't sing, but they can fly. They live in nests and steal food from people.

The **centaur** is part horse, but it's got the head and top half of a man, and the body and legs of a horse.

Sometimes people think **mermaids** are the same as sirens, but mermaids are half woman, half fish. They've got beautiful long hair, but they haven't got legs. They've got a fish's tail with scales.

2 Read again and say 'yes' or 'no'. Correct the wrong sentences.

1 Griffins make their nests from feathers.
2 A dragon's got the body of a lizard.
3 A centaur's got the legs of a goat.
4 A unicorn's got two horns.
5 Sirens and harpies are part dragon and part woman.
6 Sirens steal people's food.
7 Harpies live in nests.
8 Mermaids have got a big lizard tail.

3 Talk to your partner.

1 Which of these beasts do you think are the most interesting? Why?

I think griffins are the most interesting because they make nests from gold.

2 Can you think of another beast from a story you know? What does it look like?

A cyclops is a giant with one eye. It looks like a very big man!

1 Listen and choose the right words. (8)

1 The phoenix is a **song** / **myth** / **game**.
2 The phoenix was a beautiful **bird** / **lion** / **horse**.
3 The phoenix lived for **five** / **fifty** / **five hundred** years.
4 The first people to believe in the phoenix were the **Egyptians** / **Romans** / **Greeks**.
5 The phoenix was born in a **pond** / **fire** / **tree**.

2 Read and complete. Order the pictures.

clearer do Fleece Greece horse island sea sings song sports ~~told~~

Myths and legends, stories of old,
Beastly tales which people (1) told.
Adventures and monsters, strange animals too,
Heroes who had great things to (2) ______.

The Greeks are famous, not just for (3) ______,
But also for Jason and the Argonauts.
They wrote, in their mythology,
Of his adventures across the (4) ______.

Jason's bad uncle made him look for the 'fleece'.
Special wool made of gold, so they tell us in
(5) ______.

He had a clever teacher, like yours, of course!
His teacher was a centaur – half man, half
(6) ______.

The teacher told him all about the dangerous siren
Who could break his boat on rocks round the
(7) ______.
She's half woman, half bird, with feathers and wings.
She sounds really beautiful when she (8) ______.

The Argonauts were sailing and before too long
They started to hear the siren's (9) ______.
It sounded lovely, but they didn't go nearer
'Cos Orpheus's music was louder and (10) ______.

This is part of the myth from Ancient Greece
Of Jason and the Golden (11) ______.

a

☐

c

☐

b

1

d

☐

e

☐

3 Listen and check. Then do karaoke. (9–10)

4 Invent an amazing mythical beast. Answer the questions.

1 What are you going to call it?
I'm going to call it a …
2 What's your beast going to look like?
It's going to have a …'s head, …
3 What colour's it going to be?
4 Is it going to have feathers, fur or scales?
5 Is it going to have spots or stripes? What else is it going to have on its body?

5 Ask and answer about your beast in pairs.

6 Draw and write about your beast. Write 30–40 words.

Sounds and life skills

Supporting your friends

1 Watch the video. How does Stella feel before, during and after the audition?

Pronunciation focus

2 🎧 11 **Listen and write the word endings. Then practise with a partner.**

LENNY: Well, I think you're good at sing_____!

STELLA: I'm go_____ to be a famous writer, start_____ with that blog competition! So, what are we going to write about this time?

LENNY: Well, not **The K_____ of the Beasts**!

MEERA: … there are some older stories about other really excit_____ beasts.

3 🎧 12 **Listen and write. Say some more examples.**

I think you're good at __________ __________.

Are you __________ to __________ in a competition?

4 🎧 13 **Listen and number. What other support can you give?**

What do you worry about?

a 

b 

c 

d 

5 **In pairs, do a role play.**

Student A
You are worried about something. Tell your partner.

Student B
Listen to your partner. Give them some support.

Useful language

Good luck with …
Go for it!
You're good at it!
We're right here with you!

Diggory Bones

14

1 **Why is Iyam Greedy a bad pirate? Which god in Aztec mythology was part bird and part snake?**

How have our toys and games changed?

1 15 **Listen and read. Which toys or games do people still play with today?**

Fun and games in ancient times

Did you know that people in **ancient** times loved playing with toys and games just like we do today? In fact, many toys and games from the past are **similar to** modern ones. So how did people have fun a long time ago?

One of the oldest board games in the world is called Senet and it was very **popular** in ancient Egypt. Can you believe that people enjoyed playing it more than 4,000 years ago? Some people used a box with 30 squares and **counters** made of **bone**, but there were other ways to play it. Some people made their own game by drawing squares in the sand or on paper and using stones as counters, so it was a game for everyone.

The Ancient Greeks and Romans played games with **dice** made of bone, wood or stone. The dice had six sides with spots on them to show the numbers, just like dice today. Some very early dice had only four **sides**, which were in the shape of a triangle. The oldest dice ever are about 5,000 years old!

People started playing with yo-yos more than 2,000 years ago. This painting shows a young Greek woman with a yo-yo. They were often made of wood, metal or **terracotta**, and they had a string attached.

2 **Read again and complete the table.**

Toy/Game	Place	Time	Materials
(1) yo-yos	ancient Greece	2,000 years	(2) ________, metal, (3) ________, string
board game	(4) ________	(5) ________	bone, or sand, paper and (6) ________
(7) ________	(8) ________ and ancient Rome	5,000 years	bone, wood, stone

3 **Which toys or games did you like when you were young? What entertainment is popular today?**

I loved playing board games when I was young, but I like video games now.

I think playing games on a smartphone is really popular today!

FIND OUT MORE
What are some other games people played in ancient times?

1 Read the review. How do you win this game?

DID YOU KNOW...?
Monopoly is one of the most popular board games in history and more than one billion people in the world have played it! The longest Monopoly game ever took 70 days!

Blog | Game on! | Index

Cluedo ★★★★★

Cluedo is a classic board game which families have enjoyed since 1949! Everyone is a detective, and the winner is the player who solves the murder of Doctor Black. You need to use logic to discover the name of the murderer, the weapon they used, and the room where the murder happened.

The game has got a board with a big house on it. Players use dice to move around, and when they are in a room, they can make guesses about the murderer, the weapon, and where the murder happened. You can use logic to work out the correct answers. It's a game which usually takes between 10 and 60 minutes – not too long and not too short!

To play Cluedo, you need 3–6 players who are aged 8 or older. This makes it a perfect game for having fun with your family and friends.

I think every house should have Cluedo on their games shelf because it's great fun and it helps you practise your problem-solving skills at the same time.

by Eliana

2 Underline **who** and **which** in the review in Activity 1.

3 In pairs, discuss a game you know how to play. Answer these questions.

- How do you play the game?
- How long is it?
- How many players do you need?
- How old should they be?
- How do you win?
- Why do you like the game?

Learning to write: *who and which*

We use **who** and **which** to connect two parts of a sentence.

Cluedo is a classic board game **which** families have enjoyed since 1949!

The winner is the person **who** solves the murder.

Ready to write:

Go to Activity Book page 16.

Project

Make a board game.

2 Tomorrow's world

How many types of transport do you know?

1 What does the rocket do? Watch and check.

2 Watch again and correct the sentences.

1 Meera's making a car.
2 Lenny thinks we'll travel by water.
3 The rocket will swim.
4 The rocket will go to the stars.
5 Meera will get some photos of rockets.
6 Their next blog post will be about the transport of the past.

Meera's making a rocket.

STUDY

We'**ll** all **travel** by air.
Will it **fly**?
It **won't go** very far.

3 Read and order the words.

1 the / hit / will / rocket / The / window.
2 fly? / Meera's / Will / rocket
3 stars. / won't / to / the / rocket / go / Meera's
4 will / hit? / rocket / the / What
5 another / won't / rocket / fly / garden. / the / They / in
6 transport / be / of the / future. / will / Rockets / the

4 Ask and answer.

1 Lenny thinks rockets are the transport of the future. Do you agree?
2 Do you enjoy doing science experiments? Describe your favourite one.

Language: predictions with *will*

1 Can you remember the last lesson? Watch the language video.

2 Read and say the words.

Transport of the future!

It'll be a (1)  , not a (2)  .

It'll pick up kids for school.

It'll stop for all of us.

Transport of the future!

I'll have a computer on my (3)  .

It'll say, 'Be careful!

(4)  on right!'

So I'll ride it where I like!

Transport of the future!

There won't be (5) 

or (6)  .

How'll we go on holiday?

We'll catch spaceships and spaceplanes.

Transport of the future!

We'll have wings on all our

(7)  .

Where do you think we'll go?

We'll fly up to the stars.

Transport of the future!

We'll take a (8)  to the moon.

When'll we leave planet Earth?

We'll leave here very soon!

3 16–17 Listen and check. Then do karaoke.

4 Read and answer.

In the future we won't drive on roads and motorways. We'll use carplanes, which will fly three metres above the ground. These will carry six people. They won't have a pilot because a computer will fly them. There'll be a small round table and six armchairs with cushions inside, like a small living room. There'll be a robot waiter to give us food and drink. We'll chat on the internet and watch our favourite videos on big computer screens.

There won't be any normal doors. The sides of the carplane will open by moving slowly down under the floor of the car. There won't be any maps and we'll never get lost because carplanes will always know where to go.

1 What transport will we use in the future?
2 How high will carplanes fly?
3 Why won't a carplane have a pilot?
4 What kind of chairs will there be inside?
5 What will the inside of a carplane look like?
6 Why will it be easy to travel without maps?

5 Do you think these things will happen? Why or why not?

In 2075 …

1 people will eat different food.
2 children won't need to go to school.
3 everyone will have a robot which looks like a person.
4 no one will drive cars or trains.
5 there won't be any smartphones.
6 people will keep their memories on a microchip in their head.
7 waiters in restaurants will be robots.
8 people will wear different clothes.

6 Work in pairs. Talk about what life will be like in 2075.

I think we'll eat different food.

Really? What kind of food do you think we'll eat?

7 Write about your city in 2075. Write 30–40 words.

1 Read the blog. What are the three different kinds of space tourists?

ALL BLOGS | MY BLOG | NEW POST

Kid's Box Reports

Our next blog post is about space travel. The first man walked on the moon in 1968, but now engineers are designing rockets which will send astronauts to Mars.

Space travel

The most important space agencies in the world are NASA (in the USA), ESA (in Europe) and the Russian, Chinese and Indian space programmes. They build rockets and teach astronauts how to fly them. Rockets take a long time to build and cost a lot of money, so they're too expensive to use as normal **transport**.

A new space programme called Artemis is planning different kinds of missions which will help us to explore space. Some of these missions will take people to the moon and to Mars. The astronauts on these missions live on a giant space station called the Gateway, which will stay in space for more than ten years. On the Gateway, astronauts make and recycle **air** and water so they can live in space for a long time.

Some businessmen are helping space agencies to build better and cheaper rockets because they are interested in space travel, and they want to send **tourists** into space and to the moon. Space tourists are people who are not astronauts, but want to visit space. It's a very expensive adventure! In 2021, a Japanese billionaire **businessman** paid nearly $35 million to stay on the International Space Station for 12 days. He is called an 'orbital space tourist'

because he travelled around the **Earth**. 'Sub-orbital space tourists' can go to see Earth from above, but they don't orbit it. They fly higher than 100 km above Earth, which is where space starts, and for about five minutes they **float** inside the spaceship. One day, 'lunar tourists' will travel outside Earth's orbit. They'll travel to the moon and in the future they'll be able to go to Mars, too.

2 Read again and answer.

1 Where are the five most famous space agencies?
2 Name two problems with rockets.
3 Who flies rockets?
4 What will astronauts do while they live on the Gateway?
5 What are businessmen helping space agencies to do?
6 How much did it cost the businessman to travel round Earth?
7 How far from Earth is space?
8 Where will space tourists travel in the future?

3 Talk to your partner.

1 Do you think you'll ever travel to the moon? Why or why not?
2 Would you like to go to Mars? Why or why not?

No, I don't. Because I haven't got lots of money!

I would like to go to Mars because I love adventures.

1 Look at the pictures. Read and order the words.

1 and make / Engineers / spaceships. / will design
2 in space stations / will stay / Space tourists / for their holidays.
3 on Mars but / will work / not on the sun. / Robots
4 Rockets and / solar energy. / will use / other transport

2 18 Listen and answer. What is the man designing?

3 19 Listen again and write.

Name: (1) Robert
Surname: (2) ______
Dream job: (3) ______
Age next birthday: (4) ______
Present job: (5) ______
Rocket name: (6) ______

4 Write questions with 'will'.

1 When / go / space?
2 What kind of clothes / wear / space?
3 What kind of food / eat / space?
4 What / take / photo of?
5 Who / go with?
6 What / take / with you?

1 When will you go into space?

5 Imagine you are an astronaut. Ask and answer.

When will you go into space?

Well, I think I'll go next year.

Sounds and life skills

Choosing a point of view

1 ▶ **Watch the video. What do Lenny and Stella think about the rocket?**

Pronunciation focus

2 🎧 20 **Listen and underline the strong words. Then practise with a partner.**

LENNY: Soon there won't be any buses or cars – we'll all travel by air.
STELLA: Or we'll walk. We'll still have legs!
LENNY: Will it fly?

3 🎧 21 **Listen and complete. Practise with a partner.**

A: In the future, we'll ____________________ .
B: And we won't ____________________ .
A: Will we ____________________ ?
B: I'm not sure.

4 **In pairs, think of and write more examples.**

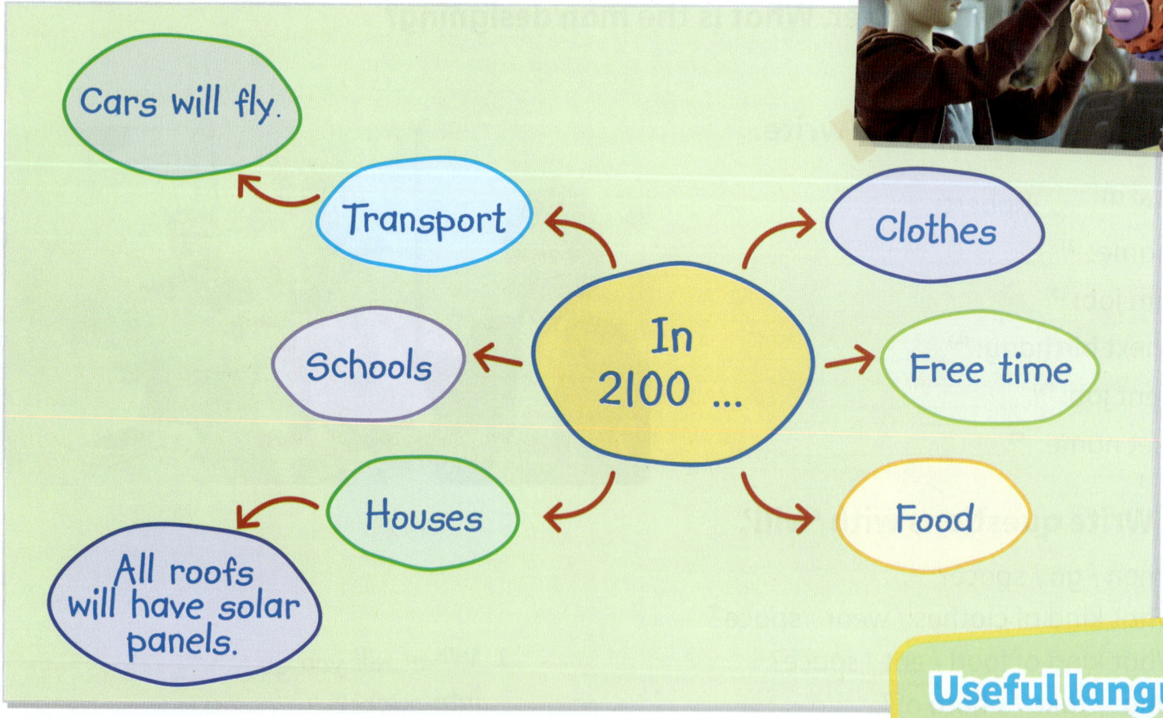

5 **In a group, discuss your predictions. Do you agree?**

I agree, I think we will …

I don't agree. We won't … because …

Useful language

In the future, I think we'll …
We won't …
I agree / I don't agree because …

22

Diggory Bones

2

1 **What did the Aztecs and the Mayas use to measure time? When did the Aztec new year start?**

What can robots do for us?

1 23 **Listen and read. What kinds of robots are in the photos?**

LIFE WITH ROBOTS

Did you know that a robot called Raptor can run 46 km an hour? That's much faster than the fastest human on Earth! Humans make robots with **computer technology** and they help us do different kinds of jobs.

In 1961, a factory in the USA used the world's first industrial robot. It was a robot arm that could pick up hot metal to make cars, which is a dangerous job that's difficult for humans to do. Robots work faster than people too, so this helps factories to **produce** more.

In hospitals, medical robots help doctors to do important jobs. For example, special machines can **perform surgery** if the doctor's hand is too large. And doctors can even do surgery from a distance. They use computers to control robots which perform **remote surgery** on people who are in a different hospital.

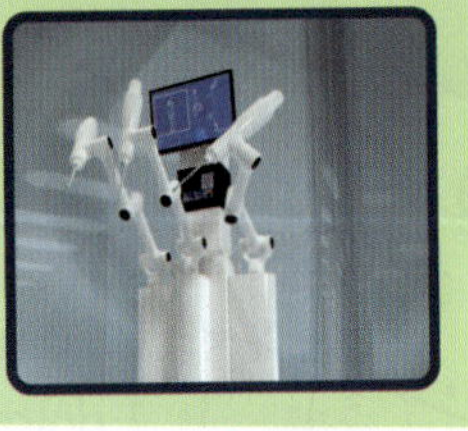

At home, a domestic robot makes life easier for humans. These robots can clean, look after your pets, or keep your home safe thanks to a **built-in alarm**. They can even **entertain** you! Some **robot devices** can answer questions, play your favourite music, and search the internet for you!

Humans have used space robots since the 1950s. The first space robot to go all the way to Mars was called Viking. Viking's job was to take photos of Mars to help us learn more about the planet. Since then, five different **robot vehicles**, called Rovers, have travelled to Mars too. These robots do lots of **research** to find out if humans will be able to visit Mars in the future.

2 **Read again and answer.**

1 Which robot would you choose to do important research for humans?
2 Which robot would you choose to help with housework?
3 Which robot would you choose to do surgery on someone?
4 Which robot would you choose to do jobs that aren't safe for humans?
5 Which robot would you choose to take photos of another planet?

A space robot.

3 **Have you ever used a robot device? What can you use it for?**

We've got a robot device at home. I can talk to it and ask it questions.

What does it say?

It tells me the time, and what the weather's like.

FIND OUT MORE
The Robobee is one of the smallest robots in the world! What does it look like?

1 Read the instructions. What kind of robot is it? Write.

DID YOU KNOW...?

Robots can travel very far from home! It took the spacecraft carrying the Perseverance Rover seven months to reach Mars. It had to travel about 480 million km to get there!

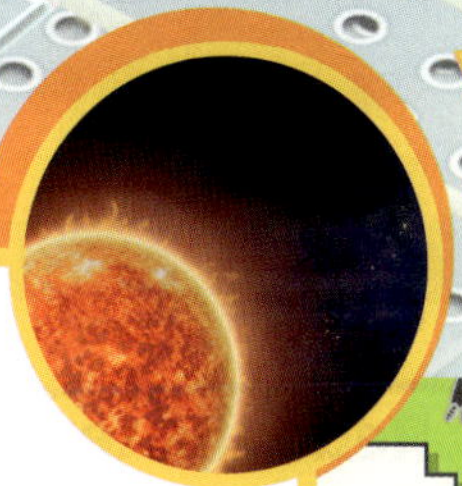

How to make a ________ robot

Materials

You will need paper, pencils, scissors and craft materials.

Instructions

1. Plan your robot. Think about your robot and answer these questions:
   - What will it do?
   - What will it look like?
   - How far will it travel?
   - How will it move in space? (Wings? Solar power?)
   - What other special things will it have? Will it have wheels, arms, or cameras to take photos?
2. Draw a picture of your robot and label all of the parts.
3. Build your robot. Use any materials you can find. If something doesn't work, don't worry. Try a different way.
4. Test your robot. It will need to land on a planet, so it will need to be strong. Shake it and check it doesn't break.
5. Give your robot an exciting name. Mars Rovers in the past were called Perseverance, Spirit, and Opportunity!

2 Underline the instruction verbs in the instructions in Activity 1.

3 In pairs, discuss ideas for a new robot. Make notes in your notebook.

Learning to write:

Instructions

We use a verb, or **Don't** + verb, to give instructions.

Plan your robot.

If something doesn't work, **don't worry**.

My Robot

what it looks like: ________

how it works: ________

what it does: ________

Ready to write:

Go to Activity Book page 24.

Project

Follow instructions and make a robot.

Review Units 1 and 2

1 Read the text. Choose the right words and write them on the lines.

The moon is (1) Earth's only natural satellite. That means that the moon (2) ________ around the Earth once every 27 days. It is (3) ________ than Earth and (4) ________ diameter is 3,474 km.

The first visit to the moon was (5) ________ 21 July 1969, (6) ________ Neil Armstrong, an American astronaut, (7) ________ the first man to walk on the moon. The USA sent rockets with astronauts to the moon over three years but they stopped in 1972 because it was very expensive.

Now different space agencies (8) ________ they will send astronauts to the moon again. The American, the Russian, the Chinese, the Indian and the European space agencies all have plans for missions to the moon. NASA (9) ________ to build a camp at one of the lunar poles. It is doing tests in Antarctica to see how well it (10) ________ . It wants astronauts to visit the moon again so it can plan to fly to Mars!

1	Earth	Earth's	Earth is
2	goes	went	go
3	more	small	smaller
4	it's	its	her
5	in	for	on
6	when	who	where
7	is	was	were
8	say	says	saying
9	can	will	wants
10	works	work	working

2 🎧 24 Listen and colour and write. There is one example.

3 Play the game.

Rocket launch

Instructions:

- English is the international language of space. USE it or MISS a turn!
- Throw a dice and move round the board. First, collect a rocket, fuel and food on Earth.
- When you have all three, continue to the LAUNCH square and fly to the moon.
- When you reach the LAUNCH square, fly to Mars. How will you help the planet?
- Read and follow all the instructions as you move round the board. Race to the END!

3 The great outdoors

What activities do you like doing in the countryside?

1 ▶ **Where did Lenny break his arm? Watch and check.**

2 ▶ **Watch again and say 'yes' or 'no'. Correct the wrong sentences.**

1 Lenny broke his arm last Friday.

No. Lenny broke his arm last Saturday.

2 Lenny was jumping when he fell.
3 Lenny was jumping over a rock when he broke his arm.
4 Lenny put his foot in a hole when he was crossing the bridge.
5 Lenny was taking his boots off when he fell over.

STUDY

I **was jumping** over a rock when I **fell**.
Were you **playing** when you **broke** your arm?
No, I **wasn't playing**.

3 **Read and choose the right words.**

1 Lenny and his dad **was** / **were** climbing a hill.
2 Lenny **was** / **wasn't** playing when he fell over.
3 They were **walking** / **walks** across a bridge when Lenny put his foot in a hole.
4 They **wasn't** / **weren't** having a picnic in the wood.
5 Lenny didn't break his arm when he **is** / **was** crossing the bridge.
6 He was **taking** / **took** his boots off when he fell over.

4 **Ask and answer.**

1 What did you think of Lenny's big adventure?
2 Have you or one of your friends ever broken a bone? What happened?

1 Can you remember the last lesson? Watch the language video.

2 Read and complete.

And I had to jump out | Go down a waterfall | It didn't make a sound | ~~There was nowhere else to go~~ | Was racing after me

I was climbing up the mountain
When it started to snow.
I hid in a cave.
(1) There was nowhere else to go.
What an adventure!

I was swimming down a river
When I thought I saw a tree.
A big crocodile
(2) ______.
What an adventure!

I was flying over an island.
I was looking all about
When my plane coughed and stopped
(3) ______.
What an adventure!

I was sailing on a river,
Enjoying it all.
Then I saw a boat in front of me
(4) ______.
What an adventure!

I was camping in the jungle.
I was sleeping on the ground,
When suddenly I felt a snake.
(5) ______.
What an adventure! What an adventure!

3 25–26 Listen and check. Then do karaoke.

4 In groups, say what happened next.

5 Play the game.

1 Listen to your teacher. Write your answer at the top of a piece of paper.
2 Fold the paper and pass it to the classmate on your left.
3 You can read the story when you answer the last question.

6 Write the story from the game.

My name's Diggory Bones.
I was on a space rocket at 4 o'clock last Saturday afternoon.
I was wearing a swimming costume and sunglasses.

1 Read the blog. Which journey do you think is the most exciting? Why?

ALL BLOGS | MY BLOG | NEW POST

Kid's Box Reports

We always want to find out more about the planet where we live. Explorers travel to new places to learn new things.

Explorers

Marco Polo

Marco Polo was not the first European to travel **east** to China, but he is the most famous because of his books. Lots of people have read these, including the explorer Christopher Columbus. Marco left Italy in 1271 and returned 24 years later. When he went to China he travelled mostly over **land**, but when he came back to Europe, he travelled mostly by sea. He brought back the idea of paper money, which people later copied.

Zara Rutherford

In 2021, Zara Rutherford became the youngest female pilot to fly around the world by herself. She began her **journey** in Belgium and flew **west**, and she stopped in 31 countries on five different continents! It took her five months to travel more than 50,000 km in a special plane called a microlight. This is a plane so small a person can push it. Because her plane was so small, she couldn't carry a lot of things with her, but she had a **rucksack**, a **sleeping bag** and a **torch** or **flashlight** to see in the dark.

Felicity Aston

Felicity Aston is another famous explorer. She began her **adventures** in 2000 when she travelled to Antarctica for the first time. She has been on **expeditions** all around the world, but especially to the **North** and **South** Poles. She skied across Antarctica alone in 2012. It took her 59 days to cover 1,744 km, so she had to **camp** in a **tent** every night. She was the first woman to do this. She has written books about her adventures and has won a lot of prizes for her work.

2 Read again and correct the sentences.

1. Marco Polo travelled east to Australia.
2. Marco Polo wrote a newspaper about his journey.
3. Zara Rutherford flew around the world with her parents.
4. A rucksack is a bag you can sleep in.
5. A microlight is one of the biggest planes in the world.
6. Felicity Aston began her adventures in 2021.
7. Felicity Aston was the first woman to snowboard across Antarctica.
8. Felicity Aston has designed computer games about her adventures.

3 Talk to your partner.

1. Which of these explorers do you think had the most difficult adventure? Why?

> I think Felicity Aston had the most difficult adventure because she skied across Antarctica alone!

2. Where would you like to explore? Why?

> I would like to explore China because I have never been there, and I like Chinese food.

1 Read and match. Say the word and the letter.

a 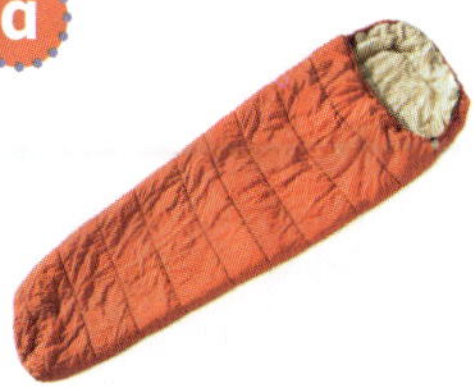
b 
c 
d 
e 

torch – d

1 It's something you use to see in the dark. ☐
2 It's a big bag which you carry on your back. ☐
3 It's like a small house. You use it when you go camping. ☐
4 It's something which you sleep in. ☐
5 It's someone who travels to a new place to learn about it. ☐

2 Look at the map and say 'yes' or 'no'. Correct the wrong sentences.

1 Clidditch is north of Ness Lake.
2 Alchester is south of the Deep Sea.
3 Mainwitch is east of the Deep Sea.
4 Hamptonville is north of Deer Wood.
5 Clidditch is south of Littleton.
6 Oldbridge is east of the mountains.
7 The mountains are south of Mainwitch.
8 Littleton is west of Mainwitch.

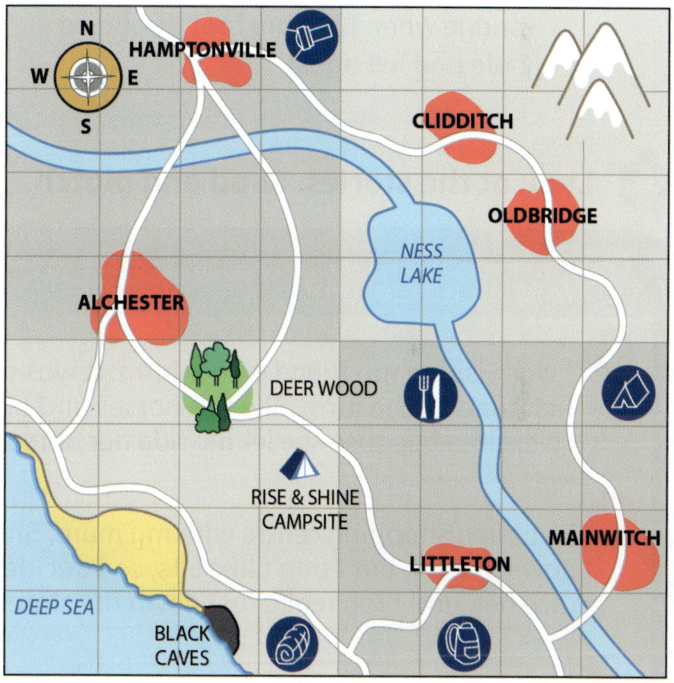

3 Play the game.

It's south of Clidditch and west of Oldbridge.

Is it Ness Lake?

Yes!

4 27 Listen. What camping things do you pick up? Where are you?

5 Write an adventure. Use the map and as many words in the box as you can.

beach bridge cave
grass hill lake
mountain plan
river rock waterfall

One day I was walking near the Black Caves by myself when ...

Sounds and life skills

Imagining possibilities

1 Watch the video. How did Lenny break his arm?

Pronunciation focus

2 28 **Listen and read. Underline the sounds /b/, /v/ or /w/.**

STELLA: So, were you playing when you broke your arm?

LENNY: No, I wasn't playing, Stella, and that wasn't when I broke my arm. We were in the wood, and we had to cross a really fast river. We were walking across the bridge when I put my foot through a hole and fell again.

3 29 **Listen and write. Practise with a partner.**

We were walking	on a ______	when I broke my arm.
	over a very fast ______	
	in a big ______	
	near a beautiful ______	

4 **Look at the stories. Read and match.**

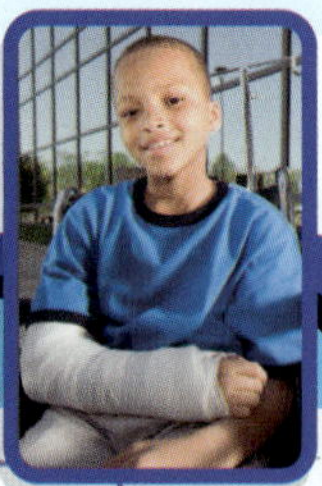

What an adventure!

1 I was visiting my friend on her farm. It was my first time on the farm. She has horses and I was so excited because she let me ride her horse!

2 I was in a shopping centre with my mum. She went down in a lift, but I don't like lifts, so I decided to race her, and I ran really fast down the stairs.

3 It was a very windy day, so I was flying my kite in the park. My kite was flying really high when it flew into a tall tree.

a I was running down so fast that I couldn't stop! I fell and broke my arm! ☐

b I was climbing up to get it when I fell and, yes … I broke my arm! ☐

c It was walking quietly when suddenly it started to go fast. I fell off and broke my arm. ☐

5 **In pairs, imagine you are Lenny and tell your story. Choose some of these places.**

How did you break your arm?

at a museum | on a camping holiday | in the park | at the funfair | in the classroom | on a farm | in the mountains

Useful language

I was (walking) when I …
We were (playing) in the park when I …

Diggory Bones

30

3

1 **What was the old name for Mexico City? Which is the highest pyramid in the world?**

What can we see in our world?

1 31 **Listen and read. Write the headings.**

Cold mountains   How are mountains formed?   The highest and the longest
The young and the old   We are mountaineers!   ~~What is a mountain?~~

1 What is a mountain?

A mountain is a **landform** that stands **high above** the land around it. There are mountains all over the world. Scientists have even found huge mountains under the sea. We call lots of mountains standing together a **mountain range**.

2 ____________________

Mountains take millions of years to form. When two **plates** in the **Earth's crust** push together over a very long time, all the rocks slowly build up and up, until they make a mountain!

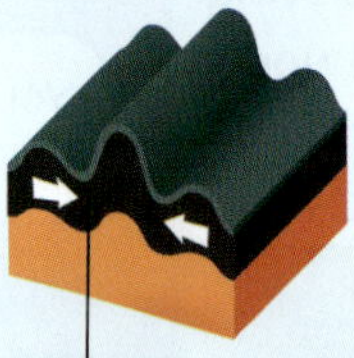

3 ____________________

The Himalayas started **forming** 40–50 million years ago. The world's highest mountain, Mount Everest, is in the Himalayas. Everest is still growing, and gets taller every year. The Himalayas are about 2,600 km long, but the Andes in South America are 7,000 km long, and they're the longest mountain range in the world.

4 ____________________

The Himalayas are millions of years old, but they are the youngest mountains on Earth. The Makhonjwas Mountains in South Africa formed about 3.6 billion years ago, and they are older than any other mountain range.

5 ____________________

Mountains are cold because they're high. Even mountains in hot countries can have snow on the top! But the coldest mountain of all is Denali in Alaska. It's the highest **peak** in North America.

6 ____________________

Lots of people love climbing mountains, and about 4,000 people have already climbed Mount Everest. But other mountains are much harder to climb. K2, also in the Himalayas, is one of the most dangerous mountains to climb because of its shape.

2 **Read again and complete the table.**

Mountain Range	Continent	Length	Age	Highest Peak
The Alps	1 Europe	1,200 km	770 million years	Mont Blanc
The Himalayas	2 ______	3 ______	4 ______	5 ______
The Andes	6 ______	7 ______	over 50 million years	Mount Aconcagua

3 **Which mountain range would you like to visit? Why?**

I'd like to visit the Himalayas, because I'd like to see Mount Everest.

FIND OUT MORE
What's the name of the highest mountain in your country?

1 **Read the profile. Why does the writer admire Malavath Poorna?**

DID YOU KNOW...?
On Mars, there is a mountain called Olympus Mons which is two and a half times higher than Everest!

3

Malavath Poorna

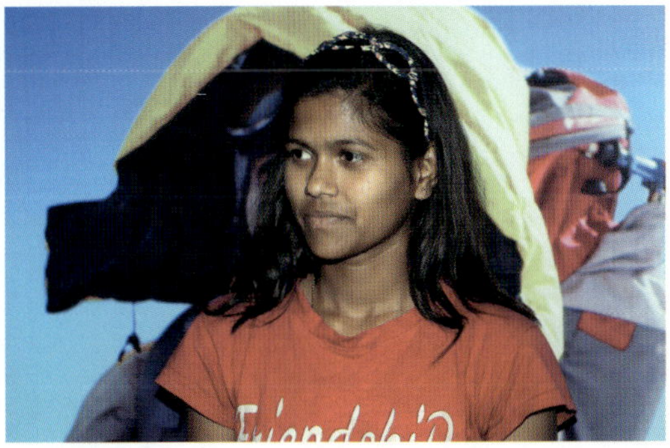

Malavath Poorna is an Indian mountaineer. I admire her because she's the youngest girl in the world to climb Everest. She was only 13 years old when she reached the top of the world's highest mountain.

She was born in a small Indian village, far away from the Himalayas. She worked hard at school and liked doing sport. One day, she was practising athletics when a teacher saw her talent. He chose her for an Everest expedition. It was a challenge, but she trained for three months to get ready to climb the mountain.

I think Malavath Poorna is very brave to do something so difficult. But she said she was never scared and wanted to make her family proud.

She likes climbing mountains on other continents too, for example Mount Kilimanjaro which is Africa's highest mountain, and Mount Aconcagua in South America.

I really like hiking, so I'd also like to climb a mountain one day. I think that to achieve something special you need to be strong and work hard to succeed.

By Lakshay

2 **Underline examples of like + ing and would like to + infinitive in the profile in Activity 1.**

3 **In pairs, discuss someone you admire. Make notes in your notebook.**

Name:
Date of Birth:
Country:
Likes:
Achievement:
Why I admire them:

Learning to write:

like + ing* and *would like to + infinitive

We use **like + ing** to talk about what we enjoy.
We use **would like** + infinitive to talk about what we want to do.

I **like climbing**. One day, I'**d like to climb** Ben Nevis, the highest mountain in the UK.

Ready to write:

Go to Activity Book page 34.

Project

Make a fact file about a landform.

4 Food, glorious food!

How many different dishes can you cook?

1 ▶ What four ingredients do you need to make tarte Tatin? Watch and check.

2 ▶ Watch again and number the sentences.

1 We've got three kilos of sugar, too. We've got too much! ☐
2 Now we haven't got enough eggs, either. ☐
3 Have we got enough flour? ☐
4 We've got too much sugar and too many apples. ☐
5 That's a kind of apple cake in French. 1
6 I think we've got too many apples. ☐

STUDY

You'll need **enough** apples to cover the base.
We have**n't** got **enough** eggs.
Have we got **enough** flour?
We've got **too many** apples.
We've got **too much** sugar.

3 Read and order the words.

1 got / apples. / a / big bag / Meera's / of
2 many / They've / apples. / too / got
3 a / They've / flour. / little / got
4 haven't / flour. / got / They / enough
5 one / only / got / They've / egg.
6 flour or / enough / haven't / They / eggs. / got

4 Ask and answer.

1 What mistakes did the children make? Why did this happen?
2 Are you good at baking? What can you bake?

1 Can you remember the last lesson? Watch the language video.

2 (32) Listen and tick (✓) the box.

1 What does Michael want in his coffee?

2 What did Paul put on the table?

3 What does Robert want on his pasta?

4 What did Mary put on the table?

5 How many pizzas did Emma cook?

3 Look and correct the sentences.

1 There are too many knives.
2 There aren't enough spoons.
3 There are too many pizzas.
4 There isn't enough milk.
5 There are too many peas.
6 There isn't enough strawberry ice cream.

4 In pairs, ask and answer ten questions with these words. Write your partner's answers.

cheese chocolate eggs fish fruit
meat pasta pizza salads soup
strawberries sweets vegetables

How often do you eat sweets?

Twice a day. How often do you eat fish?

Three times a week.

5 Talk to your partner.

I think I eat too many sweets. What do you think?

I think you eat too many sweets too, and I …

6 With your partner, tell another pair.

We think we don't eat enough fruit because we only eat fruit once a day …

1 Read the blog. How do you make jam?

ALL BLOGS | MY BLOG | NEW POST

Kid's Box Reports

People from different countries eat different kinds of food. Some dishes are famous all over the world.

Food

Sushi is a cold Japanese **dish**. You can make sushi with rice and fish which isn't cooked. You eat sushi with **chopsticks**.

In Italy they eat a lot of **pizzas** and **pasta** dishes. There are a lot of different kinds of pasta and **sauces**. Two of the most famous are spaghetti and macaroni.

Paella is Spanish. It's a rice dish, and it's also the name of the **pan** you use. People make it with chicken or seafood. It's delicious!

A **snack** is a small meal or something light to eat between meals. What's your favourite snack? The doughnut, a small ring or ball of fried dough, is famous all over the world, but it originally came from Germany and the Netherlands.

Popcorn is a healthier snack. The corn seeds make a loud noise in the pan. People ate popcorn over 2,000 years ago. Today people often eat it at the cinema with salt, or with sugar and **butter**.

Do you eat **biscuits** as a snack? In the USA biscuits are called cookies. Biscuits can have chocolate, dried **fruit** or jam in them. They have sugar too.

Peanut butter and **jam** sandwiches are popular in the USA. Peanut butter isn't made from milk. It's made from **peanuts**. We cook fruit and sugar at a high temperature to make jam.

2 Read again and say 'yes' or 'no'. Correct the wrong sentences.

1 Sushi is made from bread and sauce.
2 You eat sushi with spoons.
3 Paella is the name of a dish and a pan.
4 Doughnuts originally came from France.
5 Peanut butter and jam sandwiches are popular in North America.
6 Jam is made from fruit and peanuts.
7 'Cookie' is another word for 'biscuit'.
8 People often eat popcorn at the cinema.

3 Talk to your partner.

1 Have you ever eaten any of these kinds of food? Which is your favourite?

> I have eaten sushi, doughnuts, cookies and popcorn. My favourite is sushi!

2 What is your favourite snack and when do you eat it?

> My favourite snack is pears, and I eat one every day.

1 Read and order the pictures.

I feel hungry.
What can I eat?
Cheese and salad.
Fish and meat.

Woah, too many biscuits,
You know it's not good.
Snack on fruit and vegetables,
You know you should.

Or a big, Italian pizza.
Mmm! That's nice!
Ooh, pasta and sauce,
Or a bowl of rice.

Sushi with chopsticks?
Or cereal with a spoon?
I eat sushi with my fingers.
Let's eat soon!

It isn't time for lunch,
I know what we can do.
I'm really hungry, Dad!
I'll make a snack for me and you.

Is there enough peanut butter?
There's enough strawberry jam.
Are you going to make a sandwich?
Yes, I am.
Ooh! Thanks, Dad!

a

b

c

d

e

2 33–34 Listen and check. Then do karaoke.

3 Write four sentences. Use the words in the boxes. Play 'Food bingo'.

There's too much | There isn't enough | There are too many | There aren't enough

biscuits | burgers | butter | chopsticks | jam | olives | pasta | pepper | rice | salt | sandwiches | sausages | snacks

4 Read and choose the right words.

Last Saturday Katy decided to make spaghetti bolognese, her favourite (1) Italian pasta (2) ________ .

First, she put some cold water and some (3) ________ into a big pan to boil. When the water was (4) ________ , she put the spaghetti into it to cook.

While this was cooking, she made the (5) ________ for it. She (6) ________ some onions with meat and (7) ________ . She added some (8) ________ but she put in (9) ________ !

When it was ready she put the spaghetti onto a big plate and put the sauce on top. When she put her (10) ________ into her mouth to taste it, it was too salty and it tasted horrible!

1	French	Spanish	Italian
2	plate	dish	bowl
3	tea	jam	salt
4	hot	corn	cold
5	snack	sandwich	sauce
6	cooks	cooked	cooking
7	bananas	tomatoes	potatoes
8	sugar	salt	jam
9	too many	enough	too much
10	plate	fork	cup

5 Which meal or snack would you like to make? Tell your partner how to make it.

6 Write about your favourite meal or snack. Write 30–40 words.

Sounds and life skills

Exploring food from other cultures

1 Watch the video. How do they feel in the cookery class?

Pronunciation focus

2 35 Listen and underline the strong words. Then practise with a partner.

LENNY: So, we've got too much sugar and too many apples.
We don't have enough flour or eggs.
What are we going to do?

3 36 Listen and write. Say some more examples.

A: We're having a picnic but …
B: We've got too many ______ and too much ______.
C: And we haven't got any ______!
B: What are we going to do?

4 Look at the blog post. Do you know these foods? Where is your favourite food from?

5 In a group, discuss food from different countries. Make notes.

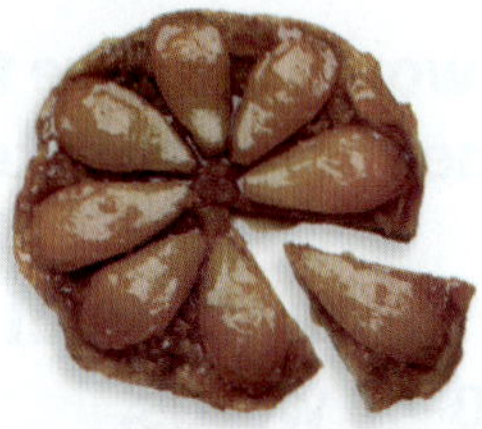

Country	Food	Ingredients
France	tarte Tatin	apples

Useful language
So let's …
Where is/are … from?
If you want, we can …
Cool, why not?

Diggory Bones

1 **Why will Diggory have to work quickly? Name three things the Aztecs ate.**

How does food get to your table?

1 38 **Listen and read. What weather do apple trees need?**

Amazing Apples

What are apples?

We all know that apples are fruit which grow on trees. They are round, mostly sweet, crunchy and delicious! In fact, apples have been part of our diet for thousands of years, and it's easy to understand why. We can eat them **raw** as snacks, and use them to make juice, sauces, desserts and salads. They taste amazing and they're very healthy, too. Apples are full of **vitamins** and **minerals**, and a lot of these vitamins are in the **skin**, so don't peel your apples!

Where do apples grow?

Apples grow in a **mild** climate. This means they need warm summers and cool winters. The first apple trees grew in Central Asia, but now you can find them all over the world, and China is the country that produces the most apples. Farmers plant apple trees in an **orchard**, which is an area of land where fruit trees grow. Did you know there are 7,500 different types of apples around the world? Do you have a favourite type?

How do apples grow?

An apple tree grows flowers in the spring and inside each flower there are **seeds**. When insects **pollinate** the flowers, the seeds grow into apples. It takes between four and five months for the apples to be ready to eat, so **harvest time** is usually in late summer or autumn. Some countries even celebrate Apple Day around this time of year.

The next time you eat an apple, think about where it came from and how it got to you.

Apples really are amazing!

Apples float in water – this is because 25% of an apple is air!

2 Read again and match.

1 A place where fruit trees grow. [d]
2 The part of the apple that gives it its colour. [ ]
3 The time of year when fruit is ready to eat. [ ]
4 Good things in food that help keep people healthy. [ ]
5 Weather that's not too hot and not too cold. [ ]
6 New plants can grow from these. [ ]
7 To carry pollen between flowers to make seeds grow. [ ]

a vitamins and minerals
b mild
c pollinate
d an orchard
e harvest time
f skin
g seeds

3 Do apples grow in your country? How often do you eat or cook with apples?

Apples grow here – we have some apple trees in our garden.

I love baking apple cake with my grandma.

FIND OUT MORE
Why can't we eat apple seeds?

1 Read the article. Why do they move apples on water?

DID YOU KNOW...?

An apple strudel is a famous dessert from Austria. In 2016, a town in Croatia made the longest apple strudel in the world. It was 1,479 metres long, and there were 653 kilos of apples in it!

HOW DO APPLES GET TO OUR TABLE?

Apples grow in orchards in countries with mild climates. In late summer and autumn, it is time to harvest them. First, fruit pickers pick the apples and put them into wooden boxes which are called crates. Then the fruit pickers put the crates onto lorries and the lorry drivers take them to a sorting and packing building.

When they arrive, the apples float into the building on water. The water washes the apples and transports them safely so they aren't damaged.

Next, the apples pass under a scanner, which checks them for colour, roundness and damage. People use this information to sort the apples into different types.

After that, they pack the apples into new crates and store them in big, refrigerated rooms.

When they are ready for selling, people check them one last time. They put a sticker on each apple, and pack them by hand. Finally, delivery drivers deliver the crates of apples to the supermarkets in lorries.

2 Underline examples of sequencing words in the article in Activity 1.

3 In pairs, discuss where your favourite foods come from and what they are made of. Make notes in your notebook.

- Which food?
- Where does it come from?
- What do you need to do before you can eat it?

Learning to write:

Sequencing words

We use words like **first**, **next**, **then** and **finally** to show how to do something in the correct order.

First, the apples are picked.

Then the lorry drivers take them to a packing building.

Ready to write:

Go to Activity Book page 42.

Project

Write a recipe using apples.

Review Units 3 and 4

1 39 **Listen and draw lines. There is one example.**

Helen Katy Harry Michael Richard Sarah William

2 **Ask and answer.**

3 Play the game.

Snakes and ladders

Instructions: Throw a dice and move round the board. When you land on a square with words, make a correct sentence. If you are right, go UP the ladder. DON'T go down the snake. If you are wrong, DON'T go up the ladder. Go DOWN the snake.

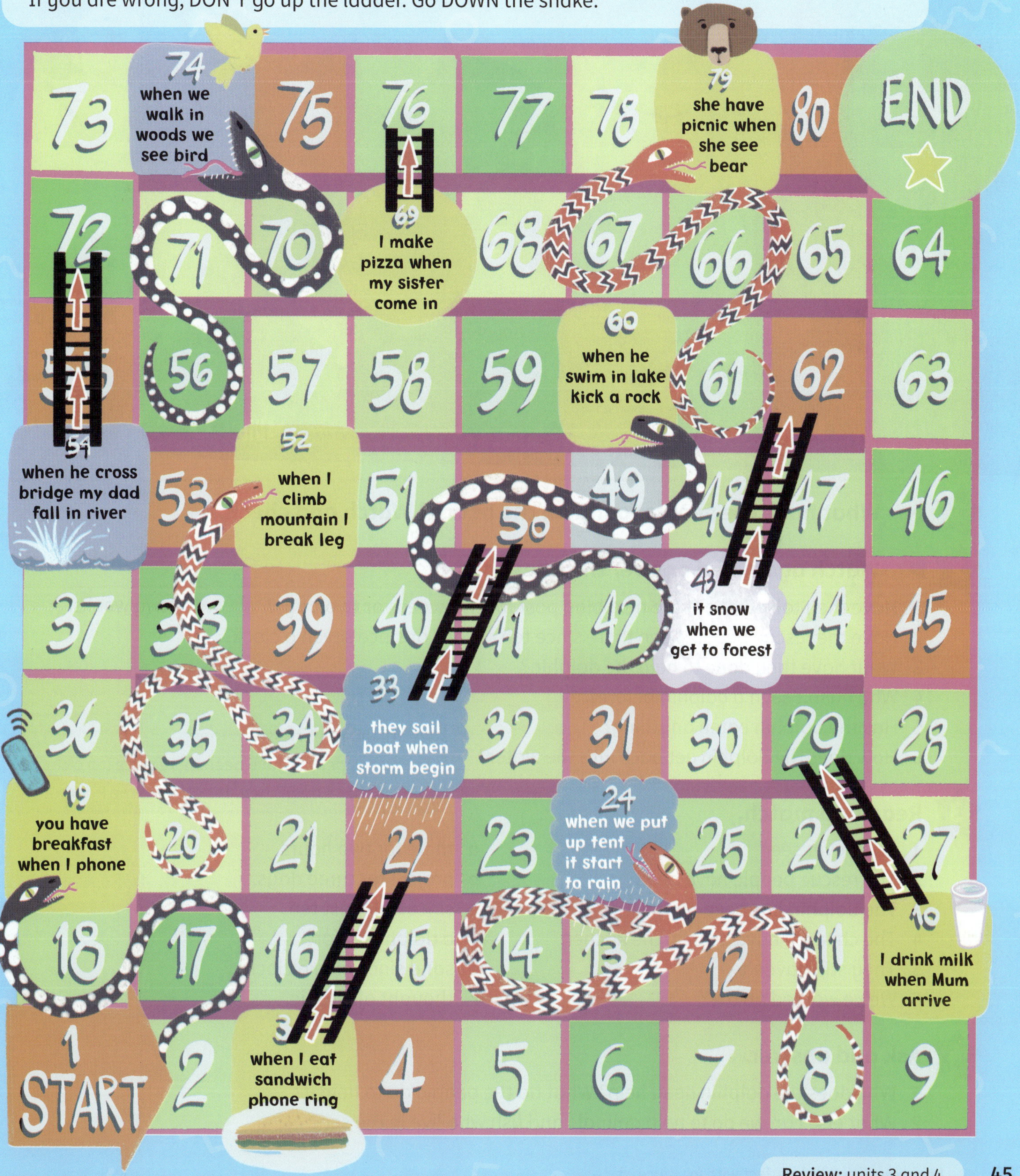

5 Under the sea

What sea animals can you name?

1 What have the people found on the beach? Watch and check.

2 Watch again and answer the questions.

1 Have they talked about the next blog post for two weeks or two days? *For two weeks.*
2 Have the rescue people been there since ten o'clock or since seven o'clock?
3 What have they done to help the dolphin?
4 Who hasn't seen a dolphin before?
5 Has the dolphin eaten anything?
6 How does the dolphin get back into the water?

STUDY

We **still haven't chosen** a topic.
The rescue people **have been** there **since** ten o'clock.
The dolphin**'s been** there **for** about three hours.

3 Read and match.

1 I've never seen
2 The rescue people have been
3 The dolphin has been on the
4 The children have been in the kitchen
5 They still haven't
6 We've worked on the

a there for two hours.
b project for three days.
c since half past ten.
d a dolphin before.
e sand since nine o'clock.
f thought of a topic.

4 Ask and answer.

1 Why does the dolphin need help? What do the people do to help it?
2 What else can we do to help animals and fish who live in the sea?

 Language: present perfect with *for*, *since*, *still*

1 Can you remember the last lesson? Watch the language video.

2 Read and look at the pictures. Tick (✓) the things he has done.

I've been at the beach since half past three.
I've picked up stones and shells from the sea.
I've walked in the water and I've touched it with my hand.
I've found rock pools and I've played with the sand.
I still haven't seen a dolphin or a whale.
I still haven't ridden in a boat with a sail.
I still haven't caught a fish to eat,
Or met a mermaid without any feet.
But I've sat on my towel, felt the sun on my face
And I've thought that this is my favourite place.
I've watched the birds as they've flown in the air.
I've eaten a sandwich, an apple and a pear.
I've swum with my friends, made castles with my dad.
It's one of the best days that I've ever had!
We've been here for hours, now it's time to go.
I love the beach, that's all I need to know.

3 40–41 Listen and check. Then do karaoke.

4 Ask and answer.

Has he played with the sand?

Yes, he has.

Has he sailed in a boat?

No, he hasn't.

5 Look at Michael's lifeline. Make ten sentences: five with 'since' and five with 'for'.

2012	2018	2019	2020	2021
was born in Manchester, England	started Queen Street School	learnt to play tennis	started to learn French	got a racing bike

1 Michael / live / in Manchester
2 Michael / study / at Queen Street School
3 Michael / play tennis
4 Michael / study French
5 Michael / have his racing bike

6 Draw and write your lifeline.

7 Tell your partner about your lifeline.

I've lived here since 2014.

1 Read the blog. How long have jellyfish lived in our seas and oceans?

ALL BLOGS | MY BLOG | NEW POST

Kid's Box Reports

We still haven't explored our seas and oceans completely, but here are some interesting sea animals of different shapes and sizes.

Sea animals

Seals live in the sea and on land, like **turtles**, but they don't lay eggs! They are **mammals**, so they have babies and feed them milk.

Coral reefs look like forests, but corals aren't plants. Each reef is millions of very small animals. The reefs are important because lots of other sea animals live there.

This giant Japanese spider **crab** has lived in the sea since the time of the dinosaurs. It's 4 m across. It has two **claws** and eight thin legs with white spots.

This blue-ringed **octopus** lives in coral reefs near Australia. It's very small (6 cm) but it's very dangerous.

Like crabs, **lobsters** have a hard **shell** and two big claws, but their bodies aren't round.

Like an octopus, a **squid** has eight 'legs'. This is a giant squid. They can be 14 m long and they have the biggest eyes in the world.

Jellyfish have been in our seas and **oceans** for 650 million years. They haven't got a brain or bones, and they can be from 2.5 cm to 61 m long! They eat small fish and tiny animals called zooplankton.

2 Read again and answer.

1. Which of these sea animals is a mammal?
2. How is a crab different from a lobster?
3. Why are coral reefs important?
4. Which sea animal has lived in the sea since the time of the dinosaurs?
5. Which sea animal can be 61 metres long?
6. Which small sea animal is very dangerous?
7. Which sea animal has the biggest eyes?
8. Name three sea animals that have eight legs.

3 Talk to your partner.

1. Which sea animal do you think is the most exciting? Why?

   I think the giant squid is the most exciting because it has the biggest eyes in the world.

2. Have you ever seen any of these sea animals? Which ones and where?

   I have seen seals on a beach, near my home.

5

1 Correct the sentences.

1 People have eaten lobsters since 2,000 years.
2 Jellyfish lived on Earth for millions of years.
3 People have find giant squid in all the world's oceans.
4 There have been coral reefs in our oceans since millions of years.
5 Scientists have found 6,000 different kinds of crab, but they still hasn't found them all.
6 Seals have swim in our seas for 22 million years.

2 42 Listen and write a letter in each box.

What is each person's favourite thing at the aquarium?

Mr Pepper b

Sarah ☐

Helen ☐

Richard ☐

David ☐

Emma ☐

a

b

c

d

e

f

g

h

3 Read the text and write the missing words. Write one word on each line.

We find coral reefs in warm (1) ___water___, usually near land. They are home to lots of different sea (2) ______, like lobsters, turtles, octopuses and jellyfish. Lots of beautiful (3) ______ live here too, like the clownfish and the parrotfish. The biggest coral reef (4) ______ the world is The Great Barrier Reef. It is in the sea near Australia. Coral reefs (5) ______ in danger because of dirty water and the things some people do. We need (6) ______ look after our coral reefs.

4 Play the game.

It's big and green. It's got a hard shell.

Is it a turtle?

Yes, it is!

Sounds and life skills

Finding out more

1 Watch the video. How do they feel when they see the news?

Pronunciation focus

2 43 Listen and complete. Underline the sounds /p/, /b/, /d/ or /ð/.

beach been Dad dolphin mother people there

MEERA: Hi (1) ________, what's happening (2) ________?

MR SHARMA: … they've found a (3) ________ on the (4) ________. The rescue (5) ________ have (6) ________ there since ten o'clock. They think it's lost its (7) ________.

3 44 Listen and match. Say more sentences with a partner.

They've found a	puzzle	in the desert.
	bat	behind a door.
	dinosaur	on the balcony.
	violin	in the village.
	feather	in the bathroom.

4 Read the news article. Match the information to the questions.

Dramatic rescue at Park Drive Beach

At nine o'clock this morning (1) on Park Drive Beach, (2) a father and his son found a dolphin. Rescue people have been on the beach (3) since ten o'clock this morning. (4) They have moved it onto a blanket and have put water over it. They think the dolphin was looking for its mother.
The rescue people have now seen the mother and (5) they are going to take the dolphin out to sea.

- Where is the dolphin? [1]
- Have they been on the beach a long time? [ ]
- What are the rescue people going to do? [ ]
- Who found the dolphin? [ ]
- What have the rescue people done to help it? [ ]

5 In pairs, do a role play.

Student A
You are a journalist at the beach. Ask questions about the dolphin.

Student B
You were walking on the beach when you saw the dolphin. Answer the questions.

Useful language
What's happening …?
They've found …
What have the … done to help?

45

Diggory Bones

5

1 **How long has Diggory known about the caves? What instructions has Mr Greedy given to Richard?**

How can we make electricity?

1 46 **Listen and read. Write the types of energy.**

For a long time, **energy** has come from **fossil fuels** like coal, oil and gas. We use fossil fuels to make electricity for our homes, schools, businesses and transport. But fossil fuels also cause **pollution**, so they aren't good for our **environment**. In fact, we now understand that fossil fuels are dangerous for our planet.

But can we get energy from other sources? Yes, of course! Energy is all around us, in sunlight, water and wind. These are natural forms of energy called **renewable energy**, which means we can keep using them for as long as we need.

We're already using renewable energy. Maybe you've seen **wind turbines** in the countryside, which create **wind energy**. When the wind blows strongly, this turns the turbines to make electricity.

Solar energy comes from the sun. If you see **solar panels** on the roof of a house, you know the house uses solar energy! Solar panels have **silicon** in them, which is made from sand. When the sun shines on silicon it creates an electric charge. This means solar panels can make electricity.

Hydro energy comes from water. Flowing water, like in a river, turns large turbines to make electricity. In fact, more than 2,000 years ago, the ancient Egyptians used water to turn big wheels to make flour.

More and more countries are starting to get their energy from nature. One day we'll only use renewable energy, and this will be much healthier for our planet.

1 ____________

2 ____________

3 ____________

2 **Read again and tick (✓).**

	Solar energy (sun)	Wind energy	Hydro energy (water)
1 It's a source of renewable energy.	✓	✓	✓
2 People can make it on their houses.			
3 It uses turbines.			
4 A material made of sand makes electricity.			
5 It's good for the environment.			

3 **Which types of renewable energy could work well in your country?**

We get lots of sunshine, so solar energy works well in our country.

FIND OUT MORE

What is geothermal energy?

1 Read the essay. Does the writer think tidal energy is a good thing?

The Advantages and Disadvantages of Tidal Energy

Introduction

Tidal energy is a type of hydro energy, which means it uses water. Our seas and oceans have tides, so the water levels go up and down twice a day. This movement of the water turns large turbines under the ocean, and this makes electricity.

Advantages

There are lots of reasons why people think tidal energy is a good idea. Firstly, it's renewable energy so it doesn't cause pollution. Another reason is we can always make this type of energy because tides don't stop moving.

Disadvantages

On the other hand, a disadvantage of tidal energy is that it's quite new. This means it's still very expensive to build the turbines and put them under water.

Ending

To sum up, I think that tidal energy will be very popular, because it will get cheaper as the technology gets better. Renewable energy is important for the future.

DID YOU KNOW...?

Iceland gets all its electricity from clean, renewable energy. It uses hydro energy and geothermal energy for electricity and hot water, and even to grow fresh vegetables!

The world's biggest tidal energy turbine is ready to go under water in Scotland!

2 Underline three topic sentences in the essay in Activity 1.

3 In pairs, brainstorm advantages and disadvantages of renewable energy. Make notes in your notebook.

Renewable energy

- Tidal energy
  - Never ends
  - Expensive
- Hydro energy
- Solar energy
- Wind energy

Learning to write:

Topic sentences

We use a topic sentence to introduce a new section of an essay.

There are lots of reasons why ...

On the other hand ...

To sum up, I think/believe/agree that ...

Ready to write:

Go to Activity Book page 52.

Project

Make a poster about renewable energy.

6 Free time

What free-time activities can you do in your town?

1 ▶ **What do they use to play table tennis? Watch and check.**

2 ▶ **Watch again and correct the sentences.**

1 Everything's dry outside.
2 There's nothing to do in the playground.
3 They've got everything they need to play hockey.
4 Someone else wants to kick the ball.
5 They have to go somewhere else to dance.
6 Now they've got something to sing about.

Everything's wet outside.

STUDY

some	any	no	every
someone	**any**one	**no** one	**every**one
something	**any**thing	**no**thing	**every**thing
somewhere	**any**where	**no**where	**every**where

3 **Read and choose the right words.**

1 **Everything** / **Nothing** is wet outside.
2 There's **nothing** / **anything** to do in the classroom.
3 There's **everywhere** / **nowhere** to play.
4 They haven't got **everywhere** / **anywhere** to play table tennis.
5 They've got **everything** / **nothing** they need to play.
6 Does **anyone** / **no one** else want to play?
7 Find **nowhere** / **somewhere** else to play.
8 Go outside, **everyone** / **no one**!

4 **Ask and answer.**

1 What did you think of Meera's game? Would you like to play it?
2 Have you ever invented a game? What were the rules?

1 Can you remember the last lesson? Watch the language video.

2 Read and choose the right words.

from: alex360@kidsbox.mail

Dear Robert

Last Saturday my family decided to go (1) somewhere / anywhere different for the day. (2) **Something / Someone** who works with Dad told him about an exciting new exhibition at the Space Museum. I'd like to be an astronaut when I grow up, so I want to learn (3) **everything / nowhere** about space. The exhibition was really interesting. There were (4) **some / any** different spacesuits which we could try on, but we didn't because there wasn't enough time and we wanted to go to the space cinema. We saw an old film called **Space Jam**. It was really funny and (5) **nothing / everyone** loved it. After the film, we visited the museum shop. We saw models of the Saturn Rocket, but we didn't buy one because there was (6) **no one / anywhere** there. Here's a photo. Have you ever seen it in films?

There was too much to see in one day, so we couldn't see (7) **anything / everything.** At the end, we were tired and there wasn't (8) **anything / anywhere** to sit down, so we went to the restaurant. We had (9) **no one / something** to drink before the museum closed at half past five. It was a great day out. What about you? Did you do (10) **anything / everyone** interesting last weekend?

All the best

Alex

3 47 Listen and write.

Kind of programme: (1) quiz show

The two children's names:

(2) ________ and (3) ________

The place: somewhere in the (4) ________

The place: (5) ________

How many questions does the boy ask?

(6) ________

4 Play the game. Say it in ten.

It's a sport.

Is it something you play with a ball?

Yes, it is.

Is it something you play in a sports centre?

No, it isn't.

5 Ask and answer.

Do you like playing table tennis?

Find someone who …	Name
1 likes playing table tennis.	Eva
2 goes swimming more than twice a week.	
3 has a hobby different from yours.	
4 can ski.	
5 likes skating.	
6 goes somewhere different from you in their free time.	

1 Read the blog. How long has Katy had her skateboard?

ALL BLOGS | MY BLOG | NEW POST

Kid's Box Reports

This month we've talked to different people about their hobbies.

Hobbies

Fahad enjoys **clothes design**. He makes amazing T-shirts and lots of his friends ask him to make T-shirts for them. He **sews** and paints the T-shirts.

Katy's had her **skateboard** for two years and she can do lots of exciting **tricks**. She goes to the skateboard park to practise jumping with her friends because you should never skateboard near the road.

Emma's ridden a bike since she was five. She rides her **mountain bike** everywhere, but she enjoys it best when she and her dad go to a special **bike trail**. They can cycle up and down hills and through woods.

Holly loves doing **puzzles** and playing **board games**. She plays **chess** in the school club and she's practising for a national competition. People have played chess for more than a thousand years.

Peter loves music, but he doesn't **play an instrument**. He uses his mouth to copy the sounds and rhythms of drums. This is called **beatbox**ing.

Leon has to be very fit and strong because he is a **ballet dancer**. He doesn't just dance, he must learn to jump in different ways and land safely and beautifully. He also has to lift his partner.

2 Read again and find these things.

1 something you can wear
2 something you stand on to ride
3 something you sit on to ride
4 somewhere with a lot of trees
5 somewhere you can go to ride
6 something that people have played for centuries
7 something ballet dancers must learn to do
8 someone who jumps beautifully to dance

3 Talk to your partner.

1 Have you tried any of these hobbies? Which ones?

> Yes, I have tried playing board games and beatboxing.

2 Which hobby do you think is the most difficult? Why?

> I think ballet dancing is the most difficult because you have to lift your partner.

1 Read and complete.

beatbox bike chess climb cut design everyone ~~hobbies~~
learn park sing ski something somewhere watch

Free time, free time. Lots of (1) hobbies to do.
There's something for (2) ______. There's (3) ______ for you.

You can do anything in your free time.
You can learn to skate, you can learn to (4) ______.
You can skateboard in a (5) ______ or (6) ______ in the snow.
You can (7) ______ some clothes: draw, (8) ______ and sew.

You can learn to play (9) ______ if that's what you like.
You can learn to sail or ride a mountain (10) ______.
You can learn about music: play it or (11) ______,
Pop, rap or (12) ______. Enjoy everything.

You can (13) ______ films or act in a play.
You can walk in the hills and (14) ______ to find your way.
You'll have (15) ______ to go and something to do.
You'll make new friends who like the same things as you.

Chorus

2 48–49 Listen and check. Then do karaoke.

3 Invent another verse. Use these words or your own ideas.

camp cars cook dance golf hockey make mix planes
play football / baseball sledge surf swim take photos tennis weigh

4 Read the definitions. What hobby is it?

1 This is something you can do in your free time. You do it with a board which is usually made of wood, and you can do it in a special park.

2 This hobby is a type of music, but it isn't singing. You play music without an instrument. You use your mouth and your body to make the sounds.

3 You can play this anywhere but you need a board and pieces. People usually sit down when they play this.

5 Write more definitions for your partner to guess.

It's something ...
Everyone can ...

Sounds and life skills

Imagining and inventing

1 Watch the video. How and why do Lenny's feelings change?

Pronunciation focus

2 50 Listen. Which question is more polite?

MEERA: Stella, can I please borrow a book?

BOY: Stella, can I please borrow a book?

3 51 Listen and complete. Practise with a partner. Say some more examples.

A: Can I borrow your ______________, please?

B: Yes, __________ __________ __________.

A: Thank you.

4 Read the blog. How many game ideas are there? Circle what you need.

If you can't think of anything to do on a rainy day, invent your own games!

BOREDOM BUSTERS!

We used some books for a net and two books for bats to play table tennis! But you can invent your own games! Play boot basketball, for example! Find some old boots and write numbers on them. Then, throw bottle tops into the boots and score points! Or … use your boots for a boot throwing competition outside! How far can you throw them?

Happy inventing. Have fun!

5 In a group, discuss ways to use old things. Make notes.

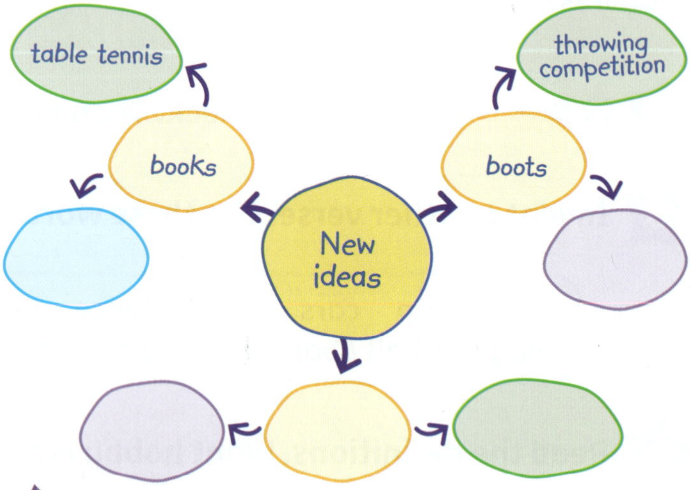

6 Compare your ideas. Choose a game to demonstrate.

Useful language

I've got an idea! We can use … to …

…'s invented a game.

52

Diggory Bones

6

1 **How often can you see the form of a snake on the north stairs? When does the pyramid sound like a bird singing?**

What makes a funfair ride exciting and safe?

1 53 **Listen and read. Label the photos.**

ALL BLOGS | MY BLOG | NEW POST

Riding the Rollercoaster

harness loops track ~~train~~ wheels

Rollercoasters are the most exciting rides at a funfair. They carry you along on a fast **train**, throwing you around and making you laugh and scream. They're so much fun!

But how do rollercoasters move? Rollercoasters use **gravity**, which is the force that pulls everything down to the ground. Rollercoasters always start with a hill. A motor pulls the train up slowly on a long, straight **track**. After the train reaches the top of the hill, it doesn't use a motor, and gravity takes control. Gravity pulls the train downwards, and whoosh! The fun starts!

Rollercoasters are fast, with **twists** and **turns**, and some have got **loops** too, which take you **upside down** for even more scary fun! But how does the train stay on the track?

If you look carefully at a rollercoaster's **wheels**, you will see that there are wheels under the track as well as on it, so they lock the train to the track. This means the train can't **fall off**.

Rollercoasters are designed to be scary, but they are actually very safe. Rollercoaster designers understand how to use gravity to push our bodies safely. Also, everyone on a rollercoaster must wear a **harness** to hold them into their seat. This is especially important when you think about the world's fastest rollercoaster in the UAE, which travels at 240 km an hour!

1 train ______

2 ______

3 ______

4 ______

5 ______

2 **Read again and order the stages of a rollercoaster ride.**

a At the top of the hill, the motor stops moving the train. ☐
b When the energy from the hill is finished, the train stops, and the ride is over. ☐
c First, a motor makes the train move up a big hill. 1
d The train travels so fast that it can even go around loops! ☐
e Gravity pulls the train down the other side of the hill very fast. ☐

3 **Do you like rollercoasters? Why? Where is your favourite rollercoaster?**

I love rollercoasters because I love going fast!

Me too! Going fast is very exciting!

FIND OUT MORE
What's the longest rollercoaster in the world? Where is it?

1 **Read the story. Does the writer like rollercoasters?**

DID YOU KNOW...?

The American engineer who designed the first steel rollercoasters hated the rides he designed because he was always sick when he rode on them!

My first Rollercoaster Ride

Last summer, I visited my cousins and the most exciting thing we did was go to a fantastic theme park. It was much bigger than a funfair and we rode on lots of great rides, like the scary ghost train and the big wheel.

After a while, my cousins asked if I wanted to ride on the rollercoaster. I said yes, but really I felt scared about it. We all sat down and put on our harnesses. Then the little train started moving slowly up a big hill. The noise of the little train moving up the high track made me feel terrified, and I just wanted to get off. When we reached the top, there was a lovely view of the theme park. It looked beautiful! Suddenly, the train dropped down the other side and everyone screamed! It was amazing! We twisted and turned, and even went upside down!

Finally, the ride was over, and we were all happy. I rode on the brilliant rollercoaster three more times that day, and now rollercoasters are my favourite rides.

2 **Underline the adjectives in the story in Activity 1. What difference do they make to the story?**

3 **In pairs, describe your favourite rides. Make notes in your notebook.**

Ride	What does it do?	How do you feel?

Learning to write:

Adjectives

We use adjectives to make stories more interesting.

The rollercoaster was **fast** and **exciting**.

I felt so **happy**.

Ready to write:

Go to Activity Book page 60.

Project

Design a funfair ride.

Review Units 5 and 6

1 Read the email and write the missing words. Write one word on each line.

Dear Yousef

How are you? In your last email you asked me about my (1) ___hobbies___ so I'm going to tell you about two of them: chess and my mountain bike.

I've played chess (2) ______________ four years now. I play with my friends at a club at school. We meet twice a week (3) ______________ Tuesdays and Thursdays. I really (4) ______________ it because you have (5) ______________ think a lot and because there's a lot of action.

My other hobby is (6) ______________ my mountain bike up the bike trails near our house with my brother. I've included a picture of me on my bike.

Tell me about some of your hobbies.

Best wishes

Joshua

2 Look at the pictures. Tell the story.

1

2

3

4

5

3 Play the game.

Can you make a question?

Instructions: Throw a dice and move round the board. You must win three verbs in a line:

To win a verb, make a correct sentence using the verb in the present perfect tense.

When you get a verb, cover it with a piece of paper and write your sentence down.

I've visited Granny twice this week.

You can land on a square that someone else has won, but you can't win it too!

40 dance	39 sail	38 snow	37 	36 comb
31 ski	32 dream	33 plant	34 email	35 
30 post	29 burn	28 	27 finish	26 jump
21 	22 invite	23 arrive	24 rain	25 mix
20 tidy	19 glue	18 brush	17 paint	16 
11 shop	12 	13 study	14 score	15 race
10 drop	9 sledge	8 text	7 open	6 start
1 play	2 smile	3 	4 visit	5 kick

7 Fashion Sense

What clothes do you wear at the weekend?

1 Why does Lenny look like a teacher? Watch and check.

2 Watch again and say 'yes' or 'no'. Correct the wrong sentences.

1 There's going to be a school trip this week.
2 Meera might wear jeans to the disco.
3 Stella's going to wear her new skirt.
4 Meera thinks Lenny might want to change his trousers.
5 Lenny's clothes may look better with a jacket.
6 It isn't cold. Lenny might not need a jacket.
7 Stella feels like a rock star.
8 They decide to write about films and music for the blog post.

No. There's going to be a school disco this week.

STUDY

I think it **may** look better with a jacket.
You **may** feel like a rock star.
I **might not** need a jacket.

3 Read and order the words.

1 might / a / Meera / T-shirt. / wear / jeans and
2 jacket? / wear / Who / a / might
3 not / wear / I / a sweater / tonight. / might
4 hot / may / a jacket. / be too / It / to wear
5 a shirt. / Lenny / wear / might
6 lot in / They / the disco. / might / dance a

4 Ask and answer.

1 What did you think of Lenny's fashion choices? Did you like any of his clothes?
2 What clothes might you wear to a school disco or party?

Language: possibility with *may*, *might*

7

1 Can you remember the last lesson? Watch the language video.

2 Look at the pictures. Read and match.

a I'm sorry, Peter. We may not have time. I've got a lot to do this afternoon.
b I don't know. I might wear my coat or I might wear my jacket.
c I think I might, or I may wear a skirt.
d She says she might come, but she needs to finish her homework first.

3 Practise the conversations with your partner. Write another conversation together.

4 Write questions with 'might'.

1 When / go / disco?
2 What clothes / wear / disco?
3 What music / dance to / disco?
4 Who / take / photographs of?
5 Who / go with?
6 What / take / with you?

1 When might you go to the disco?

5 Ask and answer.

When might you go to the disco?

I think I might go next week.

6 Play the game. What's in the bag? Write sentences with 'may'.

It may be a scarf.

1 **Read the blog. What two things did people do differently a long time ago?**

ALL BLOGS | MY BLOG | NEW POST

Kid's Box Reports

Fashions may come and go, but some fashion extras haven't changed for centuries.

Fashion

Buttons hold clothes together and **decorate** them. Today buttons are made of plastic, metal, glass and shells, but the Ancient Greeks had buttons made of gold.

Did you know that the first **umbrellas** **protected** people from the sun? Now there are big golf umbrellas and small, **light** umbrellas which we can carry in a handbag.

Your grandfather probably wore **shorts** at school until he was 12! These days we usually wear them for sport and when it's very hot.

People usually wear **gloves** on their hands when it's cold, but some people use gloves at work, for example fire fighters.

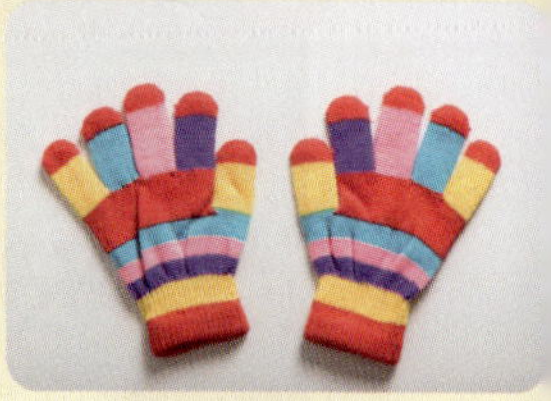

Men and women have worn **belts** for about 5,000 years. People first used them to carry things and, much later, to hold their trousers up.

The first **pockets** were small bags which people wore on their belts. Thieves could take them easily so people put the bags inside their clothes. Then it was difficult to get money out, so in the 18th century people sewed pockets into their clothes.

Women and girls wear **tights** under their skirts and dresses to cover their legs in cold weather. Tights can be **thin** and light or **thick** and **heavy**. They are usually made of **nylon** or wool.

2 **Read again and complete.**

1 The Ancient Greeks had gold buttons.
2 The first umbrellas protected people from the ______ .
3 Older boys wore ______ to school 60 years ago.
4 ______ protect our hands.
5 People wear ______ to hold their trousers up.
6 The first pockets were small ______ .
7 People sewed ______ into their clothes 300 years ago.
8 ______ are usually made of nylon or wool.

3 **Talk to your partner.**

1 Which clothes do you prefer when you want to be comfortable?

I prefer jeans and a T-shirt when I want to be comfortable.

2 Which clothes do you think are the most fashionable?

I think jeans are the most fashionable.

 Vocabulary: fashion and adjectives

1 Read and match.

1 It's very hot today.
2 My trousers are falling down.
3 Look at those black clouds.
4 I can't find my money.
5 Hey, I like your striped tights!
6 The cook's got really big gloves.

a They stop her burning her hands.
b He's wearing a T-shirt and shorts.
c They look great with that skirt.
d I need a belt!
e It isn't in my pocket!
f I might take my umbrella.

2 Read and say the words.

There's a great new dance
And we do it at school.
School disco! School disco!
Turn to the  **.**
Turn to the  **.**
Turn round and round.
Dance  **and**  **.**
School disco!

Long striped ,
Big spotted .
 and ,
And beautiful .
 and ,
 and ,
Walking out
Like queens and kings.
School disco!

Big square ,
 and ,
 and .
The clothes which we love.

Chorus
School disco!

3 54–55 Listen and check. Then do karaoke.

4 Play the game. Who is it?

He's wearing grey shorts.
It might be 'i'.
No! He's wearing …

Sounds and life skills

Planning together

1 Watch the video. How is Lenny feeling?

Pronunciation focus

2 56 **Listen and write. Then draw lines for connected speech.**

LENNY: Does this __________ OK?

MEERA: Hmm, you might want to change your shirt …

LENNY: __________ about this?

MEERA: Yeah! __________ OK! I __________ it may look better __________ a jacket …

3 57 **Listen and complete. Practise with a partner.**

A: Let's plan __________ school disco. What does __________ think?

B: Let's put __________ __________ of balloons.

C: We might want to play music __________ .

4 58 **Look. Listen and circle.**

School disco

Place: **playground / art room**

Date: **Friday 10th May / Thursday 10th May**

Time: **7.00 – 9.00 pm / 6.00 – 8.00 pm**

Theme: **sport heroes / famous musicians**

Decorations: **gold and silver / white and black** balloons

Music: **disco / rock 'n' roll**

Food: **burritos / pizza**

5 **In a group, plan your own school disco and make notes.**

School disco

Place: __________

Date: __________

Time: __________

Theme: __________

Decorations: __________

Music: __________

Food: __________

Useful language

We might want to …

How about …?

Having orange balloons may be better.

59

Diggory Bones

7

1 **How many steps are there on each face of the pyramid? What time is the sun at its highest?**

What happens to our old trainers?

1 60 **Listen and read. Give two examples of eco-friendly trainers.**

The Journey of Trainers

Trainers, sneakers, tennis shoes, sports shoes, running shoes – whatever you call them, they're shoes which people wear for sport and fashion. But have you ever looked at your trainers and thought about where they came from?

People started wearing trainers about 150 years ago. They were more comfortable than other shoes because they had **rubber soles**. In the early 1900s, people wore trainers for sport, but by the 1950s young people were wearing trainers for fashion too.

Fashion trainers were very popular by the 1980s! New, colourful designs made trainers more popular with young people. Inventions like **Velcro** instead of **laces**, and new technology like **air cushions** made trainers more comfortable than ever!

Sustainable Trainers

Most trainers are made of materials like rubber, plastic or leather, which can take a long time to **decompose** after we throw them away. This is bad for the environment. Plastic, for example, can take more than 500 years to decompose!

Making one pair of trainers also makes about 14 kg of **carbon emissions**. So, when 24 billion pairs of shoes are made every year, that's a lot of **pollution**!

To be more **eco-friendly**, many companies are using new materials for their trainers. In some shops, you can now buy trainers that are made of **plant-based materials**, like pineapples, grapes, sugarcane, cotton and mushrooms! These materials decompose more quickly, so they're much better for the environment.

Other companies make trainers out of recycled products, like plastic bottles, old fishing nets and rubbish from the oceans.

One thing is for sure, we love our trainers! So, will sustainable trainers be our shoes of the future?

2 **Read again and correct the mistakes.**

1 The first trainers had ~~leather~~ soles. rubber
2 In the 1950s, young people started wearing trainers for sport. ______
3 In the 1980s, some trainers had Velcro instead of air cushions. ______
4 Most trainers made of plastic, rubber or leather decompose very quickly. ______
5 Eco-friendly companies want to use plastic materials to make sustainable trainers. ______

3 **Have you got a favourite pair of trainers? Why do you like them?**

I love my trainers because they've got air cushions in them, so they're really comfortable!

I've got different trainers to wear when I'm not playing sport. They're fashionable!

FIND OUT MORE
What are the most expensive trainers in the world?

1 Read the leaflet. Which parts give information? Which parts give advice?

DID YOU KNOW...?

Shoes didn't have a right or left foot in the past, both shoes were the same shape! Then in 1892, an American company started making the first trainers with a right and left foot, and they were a great success!

How to give your trainers a longer life

Do you ever think about what happens to your trainers when you throw them away? Did you know that about 90% of your old shoes finish their life as rubbish? The rubbish takes hundreds of years to decompose.

One company has a great way for using old trainers – it recycles them by cutting them up into tiny pieces and using them on sports grounds and running tracks.

Here are some ideas to make your trainers last longer:

- You could make your trainers last longer by taking them off correctly. Always untie the laces and don't step on the backs.
- Don't wear the same trainers every day – you could wear different ones.
- If your trainers are dirty, clean them with an old toothbrush.
- If they're wet, put newspaper inside to dry them.
- You could take your trainers to a second-hand shop when you've finished with them.

2 Underline examples of **could** and **if** in the leaflet in Activity 1.

3 In pairs, discuss how to give an item of clothing a longer life.

Item of clothing | What is it made of? | Ideas for giving it a longer life

Learning to write:

could* and *if

We use **could** and **if** to make suggestions or give ideas.

You **could** buy clothes made of recycled materials.

If your jeans are too small, make them into a bag.

Ready to write:

Go to Activity Book page 70.

Project

Design a pair of trainers that are good for the environment.

8 Around the world

Which countries do you want to visit?

1 Where are the other winners from? Watch and check.

2 Watch again. Order the sentences.

1 They've just given the names of the blog competition winners. ☐
2 I've just tidied my desk. ☐
3 I've started it, but I haven't finished it yet. ☐
4 Have you found any good photos? 1
5 We've just won new tablets for everyone. ☐
6 Have you two written the article on Mexico yet? ☐
7 I haven't saved the article yet. ☐
8 I've already found four good photos. ☐

STUDY

Have you **written** the article **yet**?
I **haven't saved** the article **yet**.
I**'ve already found** four photos.
I**'ve just tidied** my desk.

3 Read and match.

1 Have you spoken to your
2 I've just spent
3 I haven't met
4 I've just found out some
5 Frank's already
6 She's just sent an email

a interesting things about India.
b the new French teacher yet.
c left school.
d ten euros on a new T-shirt.
e to her sister in Japan.
f mum about the school trip yet?

4 Ask and answer.

1 Have you tidied your bedroom this week? Why or why not?
2 Have you ever won a prize? What was it for?

1 Can you remember the last lesson? Watch the language video.

2 Read and complete.

been ~~begun~~ bought done packed played put tidied

We've just finished school,
Our holiday's (1) begun .
We've (2) ________ our last exam,
Now, we're going to have fun.
We've just (3) ________ away our books,
And we've (4) ________ our desks.
So we're all going home. It's time to have a rest!

Yes, it's holiday time! Time to have a break.
Yes, it's holiday time and we're all feeling great!

We've (5) ________ in the park,
And we've (6) ________ to the zoo.
We've already (7) ________
Some summer clothes too.
But we haven't (8) ________ our suitcase
And we're going to go away
To swim in the sea and sleep and play all day.

Chorus

3 61–62 Listen and check. Then do karaoke.

4 Read and choose the right words.

Hi Sarah,

How are you? I've been in Australia (1) **just / for / already** a week now, but I haven't seen a kangaroo (2) **since / just / yet**!

We've (3) **just / yet / for** left Sydney and we're driving to the beach. We've (4) **since / already / yet** seen Sydney Harbour Bridge and the Opera House, but we haven't seen the famous coral reef (5) **yet / already / for**. We'll visit it tomorrow. I can't wait! I've (6) **yet / since / already** taken a hundred photos and we've only been here (7) **for / just / since** five days!

How are your holidays? I haven't heard from you (8) **for / since / just** we arrived here. You must tell me your news!

Love

Emma

5 Write the sentences. Put the words in the correct place.

1 (already) I've eaten breakfast.
2 (yet) I haven't done my homework.
3 (yet) Have you spoken to your teacher?
4 (just) We've been to the museum.
5 (already) They've written the blog post.

1 I've already eaten breakfast.

6 Write five things you've done. Ask your partner.

I've ...

1 flown a kite.
2 swum with dolphins.
3 ridden a horse.
4 eaten octopus.
5 drunk mango juice.

7 Tell another partner.

Juan's already flown a kite. He hasn't swum with dolphins yet.

1 Read the blog. In how many countries in the world do people speak Portuguese?

ALL BLOGS | MY BLOG | NEW POST

Kid's Box Reports

Well, this is our last blog post this year. We've won the prize to write for the international blog, so today we're going to tell you about some of the other countries in the competition.

Countries

In **India** they speak more than 24 languages, but Hindi and English are the two most important languages. **Indian** people love the cinema and in Bollywood they make more films a year than in Hollywood in the USA.

Mexico is in North America, but **Mexican** people have spoken Spanish for hundreds of years. More people speak **Spanish** in Mexico than in **Spain**. Did you know that modern chewing gum first came from trees in Mexico in the 19th century?

More tourists visit **France** than any other country: about 90 million every year. The **French** also have the most famous bike race in the world, which is called the Tour de France.

Brazil is the fifth biggest country in the world. The people from Brazil are **Brazilian**, but they speak Portuguese. Apart from in **Portugal** and Brazil, people speak **Portuguese** in five other countries.

China has the biggest population in the world. More than 1.4 billion people live there, and more people speak **Chinese** as their first language than any other language in the world. The Chinese invented paper money and fireworks.

Greece is not an island, but there are about 2,000 **Greek** islands. A lot of the words we use today, like 'mathematics' and 'telephone', come from Greek.

2 Read again and answer.

1 What happens in Bollywood?
2 How many languages do they speak in India?
3 How long have Mexicans spoken Spanish?
4 Which country gets the most visitors?
5 What is the world's fifth biggest country?
6 What did the Chinese invent?
7 How many Greek islands are there?
8 Which old language gives us modern words?

3 Talk to your partner.

1 Which of these countries would you like to visit? Why?

> I would like to visit Mexico because I can speak Spanish and I love Mexican food.

2 Talk about somewhere nice to visit in your country.

> Barcelona is a great city to visit because it's next to the beach and there's lots to see.

1 🎧 63 Listen and tick (✓) the countries you hear.

India	☐	
Mexico	☐	
Italy	☐	
France	☐	
Brazil	☐	
Germany	✓	Berlin
Greece	☐	
Spain	☐	
the USA	☐	
Portugal	☐	

2 🎧 64 Listen again and write the capital cities.

3 Look and answer.

1 What is the capital of Spain?
2 Which capital here is the nearest to Rome?
3 Which capital here is the furthest south?
4 Which country is Lisbon the capital of?
5 Which capital here is the furthest east?
6 How many capitals here are north of Paris?

4 Read and correct the sentences.

8

Archie Mendes is the cleverest boy in Europe. His mother's Greek, but his father's Portuguese, so he speaks both of these languages perfectly. He also speaks English, which he's spoken since he was three, and French.

He's only 14 years old but he's studied at the Sorbonne University in Paris for two years. He's just helped some engineers to design an amazing new car which goes on land and on water.

He loves travelling and he's already been to India and Mexico, but he hasn't been to Brazil yet. He's had an invitation to visit a friend, so he's going to go there for his summer holidays.

He's just come back from Bollywood, where he helped to make a new film. He likes doing lots of different things in his free time, but his favourite hobby is free running. He's just made a short video. In it we can see him running through streets and jumping from wall to wall beautifully. He knows he always has to wear special clothes to protect his body when he does this. That's what makes him the cleverest boy in Europe!

1 Archie's parents are Chinese and Portuguese.
2 Archie speaks Greek, Portuguese, Spanish and French.
3 He's spoken English since he was five.
4 He's studied in the capital of Spain for two years.
5 He's just helped some engineers to design an amazing new boat that goes on land and on water.
6 He's already been to India but he hasn't been to Mexico yet.
7 He's only 14, but he's already helped to make a car and a TV programme.
8 He's just made a short video on long jumping.

Sounds and life skills

Understanding responsibilities

1 Watch the video. How do the girls feel? Why?

Pronunciation focus

2 65 **Listen and underline the stressed words. Then practise with a partner.**

MEERA: I've already found four good photos, but I need two more. Have you two written the article on Mexico yet?

STELLA: I've started it, but I haven't finished it yet. Oh Lenny! I've just tidied my desk. Be careful!

3 66 **Listen and write. Underline the stressed words. Say some more examples.**

A: Have you ______ your ______ yet?
B: Yes, I've just ______ it.
Yes, I've already ______ it.
No, I haven't ______ it yet.

4 **Read the article. What responsibilities does David have on the farm?**

My responsibilities … on a farm in Mexico

Today we find out about the responsibilities of a farm worker.

David, what's a typical day for you?
Well, you know farmers need to get up very early to feed the animals. The cows are always hungry! We make sure we order enough food in the winter for them until spring. Every day, we milk the cows and collect the eggs from the chickens.

Do you drive a tractor?
Yes. We've got sheep, but they aren't on the farm. I drive to their fields to check they have water. Every week I help the farmer move the sheep to a different field.

Do you also pick fruit or grow vegetables?
I sometimes help in the summer, but that's not really my job.

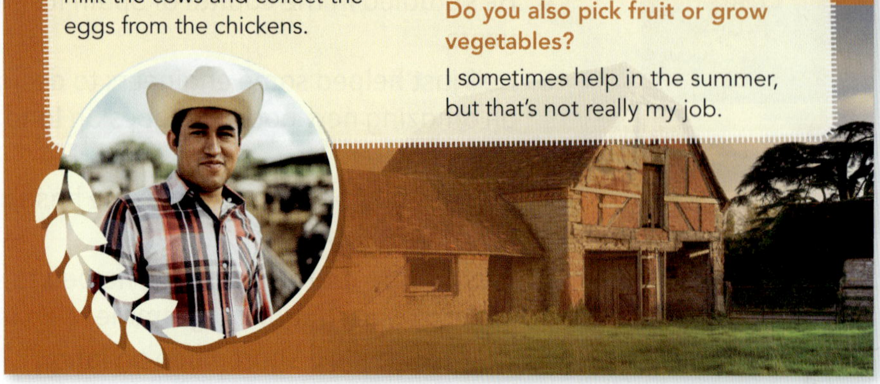

5 **In pairs, discuss different jobs and their responsibilities.**

astronaut | chef | journalist | pirate | president | teacher

Useful language

What do you do?
What's a typical day for you?
Do you have to …?
Do you need to …?

67

Diggory Bones

8

1 What has Iyam just done? How have the police found them?

Which countries do people visit most?

1 68 **Listen and read. Write 'table', 'pie chart' and 'bar graph'.**

Let's travel the world!

Do you like travelling? People travel for lots of different reasons, sometimes to other parts of their own country and sometimes even to the other side of the world!

So, what are the most popular countries for people to visit for their holidays?

Top Ten Tourist Destinations in 2019

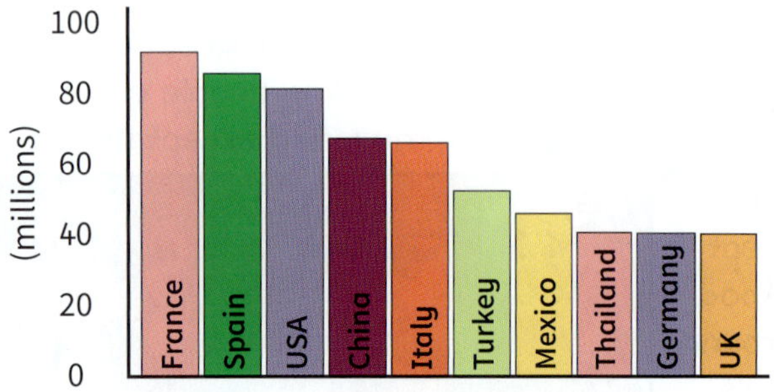

When people go on holiday, they usually enjoy going **sightseeing**, doing outdoor activities and **relaxing** on the beach. We asked a hundred young people about their favourite holiday activities.

Top Eight Most Popular Holiday Activities

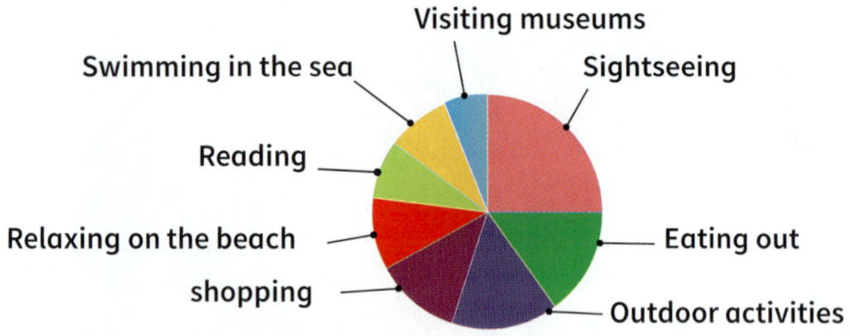

When we travel **abroad**, we usually need to use a different **currency**. The price of things is different in different countries, too. Some places are more expensive than others.

Prices in different countries

	UK	Turkey	USA	China	Mexico
1.5 litre bottle of water	95p	16p	£1.32	48p	55p
cinema ticket	£10.00	£2.28	£8.79	£5.15	£2.67
meal in a restaurant	£13.00	£2.72	£11.10	£2.33	£4.35

2 **Read again and write.**

1 The most and least popular tourist destinations. France, ______

2 The most and least expensive countries to buy water. ______, ______

3 The most and least popular holiday activities. ______, ______

3 **Which country would you most like to visit and why?**

I'd love to go to China. There are beautiful places to visit there, and the food is amazing.

FIND OUT MORE
How many tourists visit your country each year? What activities do they do?

1 **Read the blog post. What tourist attraction did Joshua visit? What activities did he enjoy?**

DID YOU KNOW...?

The Niagara Falls, which is a waterfall between the USA and Canada, is the most visited tourist attraction in the world. It has about 30 million visitors every year!

A special holiday in Greece

Last summer my grandparents and I went to Greece on holiday and I had the most amazing time. We stayed in the capital city, Athens, for three days, then we stayed on one of the islands.

Greece is a country in southern Europe which is famous for its ancient history and its beautiful islands. People live on 227 of the islands, but there are a lot more. The currency is the euro, and the official language is Greek. In summer, the weather is hot and dry.

In Athens we went sightseeing and visited lots of ancient sites. For me, the most interesting place was the Parthenon, which is almost 2,500 years old! On the island, we went to the beach and went hiking in the mountains. Greek food is delicious, and the best thing I ate was moussaka, which is made of meat and vegetables.

It was the greatest holiday ever, and I really want to go back one day!

By Joshua

2 **Underline the superlatives in the blog post in Activity 1.**

3 **In pairs, discuss a place you have visited. Make notes in your notebook.**

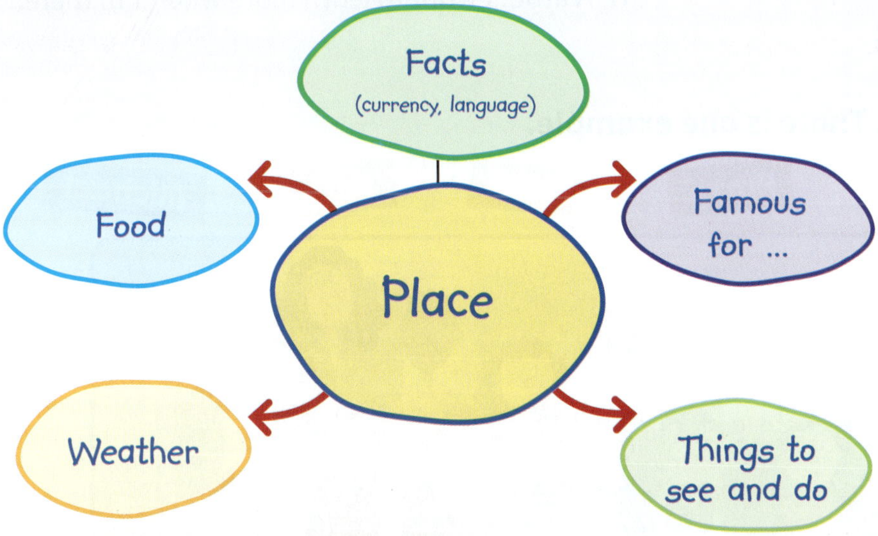

Learning to write:

Superlatives

We use superlatives to add interesting facts to our writing.

The most interesting place was the Parthenon.

Athens is **the biggest** city in Greece.

Ready to write:

Go to Activity Book page 78.

Project

Research and plan a day trip to your place from Activity 3.

Review Units 7 and 8

1 **William is talking to his friend, Sarah. What does Sarah say? Read the conversation and choose the best answer. Write a letter (A–H) for your answer.**

William: Hi Sarah, how are you?
Sarah: B
William: What are you writing in your notebook?

1 **Sarah:** ____
William: When are you going to Mexico?

2 **Sarah:** ____
William: What's the weather like in Mexico?

3 **Sarah:** ____
William: They speak Spanish in Mexico. Do you speak Spanish?

4 **Sarah:** ____
William: Have you been to Mexico before?

5 **Sarah:** ____
William: You're so lucky!

A Not yet. I went to Mexico last week.
B I'm fine, thanks.
C Never. This is the first time.
D Tomorrow afternoon. I need to get ready today.
E Very much. It's sunny most days.
F It's a list of all the things I need to take on holiday. I haven't packed my suitcase yet.
G It might be hot. So I'll have to take lots of T-shirts and shorts.
H A little. I want to learn more when I'm there.

2 69 **Listen and draw lines. There is one example.**

Betty David Emma Harry Helen Katy Michael

3 Play the game. Ask and answer.

Around the world

Instructions: Throw a dice and move round the board. Make a sentence or ask your friend a question. If you make a mistake, miss a turn.

Key

Green: Describe the picture.
Orange: *Have you ever … ?*
Yellow: *He's/She's just …*

There are four purple plastic buttons.

Have you ever won a prize?

She's just drunk tea.

Units 1&2 Values Living with technology

1 Read and choose 'yes' or 'no'. Are you A, B or C?

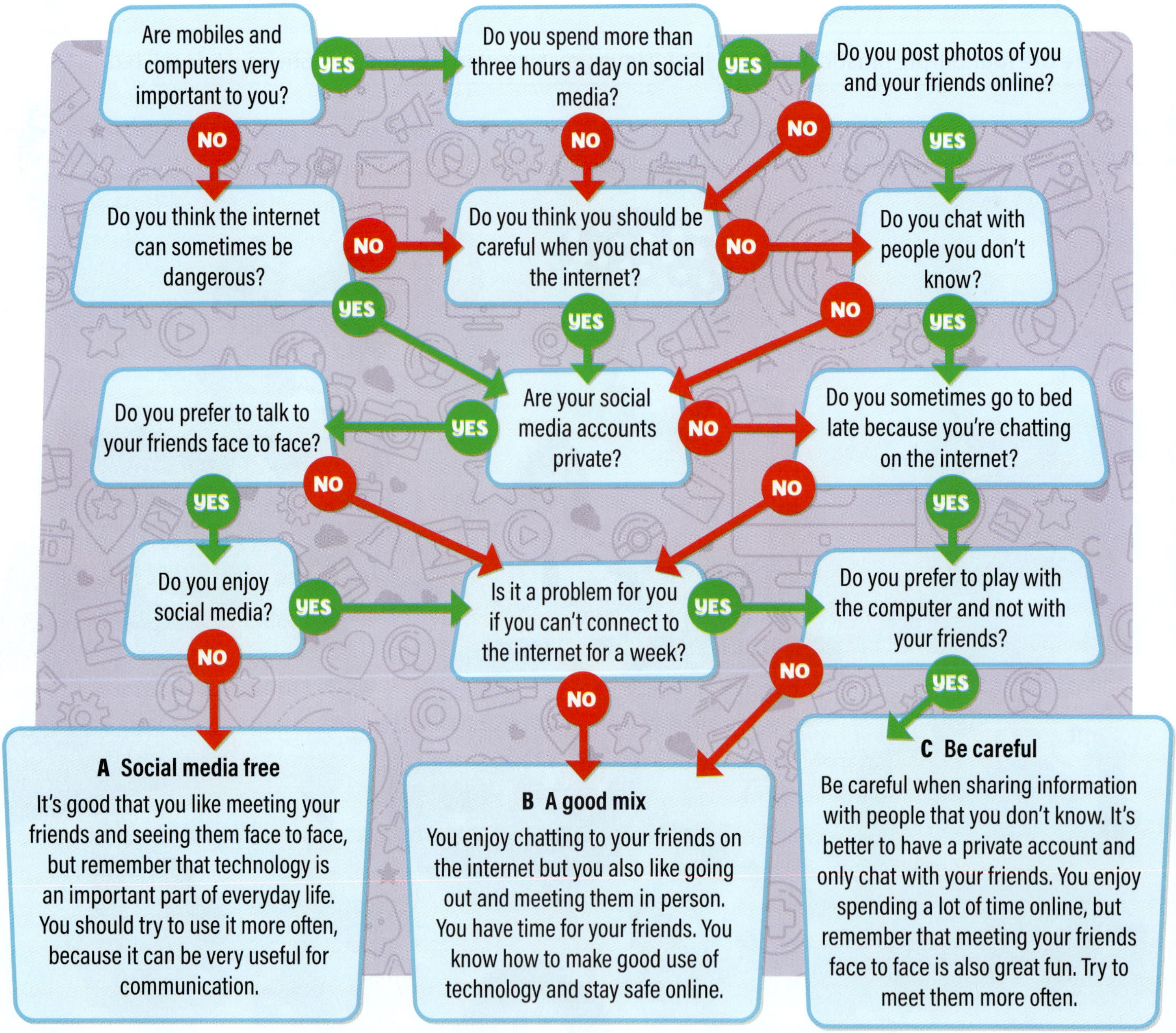

2 Do you agree with your result? Talk to your partner. Ask and answer.

1 How many hours a day do you spend online?
2 Do you think three hours a day is too much or not enough?
3 How many hours a week do you spend with your friends face to face?
4 Do you ever go to bed late because you're chatting online?
5 Why can it be dangerous to chat with people that you don't know?

Units 3&4 Values Being safe at home

1 **Look at the picture. What's wrong? What do you think is going to happen? Talk to your partner.**

Look at 'f'. She isn't sitting safely.

Yes, she's going to fall and hurt her back.

2 70 **Listen and check. Say the letter a–h.**

3 **How can you be safe at school? Write five sentences with 'should' and 'shouldn't'.**

We shouldn't walk around the classroom with scissors.
We should walk, not run, inside the school building.

Units 5&6 Values Helping at home

1 Read and answer the questions.

1 Why is Mr Banks often away from home?
2 How do the family work as a team?
3 What have Fred and Vicky learnt?

http://www.davidsreports.co.uk

David's reports

This week I've been to visit the Banks family. They all help to do the jobs around the house and to look after Mrs Banks.

David: Well, Mr Banks, can you tell us about your family and how you all work together?

Mr Banks: Yes, of course. My son Fred's 16 and my daughter Vicky's 13. We've worked hard as a family this year because my wife has been very ill.

David: Oh, I'm sorry. What do you mean when you say 'worked hard'?

Mr Banks: Well, during the year I've often been away from home. I take my wife to the hospital and I spend a lot of time there. So Fred and Vicky have learnt to do a lot of things: they sometimes do the shopping and when Fred cooks our meals, Vicky cleans the kitchen.

David: Not many children know how to cook and clean!

Mr Banks: No. Fred saw the problem and asked me how he could help at home. We spent some Saturdays in the kitchen and I showed him how to make good meals. Now he's an excellent cook! Actually, he likes to choose the food himself so he prefers to do the shopping.

David: That's great! And did you say that Vicky helps him in the kitchen?

Mr Banks: That's right. She helps in lots of other ways too. Vicky tidies the house and does the washing.

David: Well done, Vicky! How do you feel about doing all these jobs?

Vicky: Well, actually, I don't see it as extra work now. It was difficult at first because I felt that I didn't have enough time to do these jobs, do my homework and meet my friends. Now I've learnt to do things better and more quickly, so I have a bit more time. We all work as a team and I feel good because I'm part of it. I'm very lucky to have a brother like Fred. He's been great.

David: That's a nice thing to hear your sister say. How do you feel about that, Fred?

Fred: Yes, it is a very nice thing to say and I feel good, thanks. I think that before all this I was actually a bit lazy. I didn't do anything in the house and my parents had to do everything. Now I'm really happy that I've learnt to do lots of things for myself and for others. I think we're both happy to help our parents. The most important thing for us is that Mum is feeling better now.

2 71 Listen and say 'Vicky', 'Fred' or 'Mr Banks'.

3 Talk to your partner about how you help at home.

1 What do you do to help at home?
2 How can you help more at home?

Units 7&8 Values Sharing problems

1 Read the posts and answer the questions.

www.reachout-helpline.com

REACH OUT – HELPLINE

Username: TheUnicorn

Topic: Online Bullying

Last week I found my 11-year-old sister, Kim, crying in her bedroom. She told me that some other children at school have posted some horrible things about her online. She said this isn't the first time it's happened and that she's been worried about it for three weeks. She says the children who are doing it think it's funny and that it's only a joke, but she's very unhappy so she doesn't want to go to school. She's asked me not to tell my parents. What should I do?

1 Why was Kim crying?
2 How long has she been worried?
3 Do you think it's funny?

www.reachout-helpline.com

REACH OUT – HELPLINE

Username: HeretoHelp

Topic: Online Bullying

This is very serious. Your sister is very unhappy. If she doesn't want to go to school, she needs help right now. This situation has lasted long enough and it might get worse. You've listened to your sister and this has helped her, but she really needs the advice of a grown-up. You must tell your parents. It might be a good idea for them to speak to your sister's teachers. We can understand that you may feel that you shouldn't tell your parents the secret, but it's really the best way to help your sister.

4 What does Kim need?
5 What must TheUnicorn do?

www.reachout-helpline.com

REACH OUT – HELPLINE

Username: RockStar

Topic: Unfriendly Friends

An old friend has moved into the house next to mine. We've been friends since we were three, but she's a girl and I'm a boy. She's very funny and she makes me laugh, but my friends in the basketball team have started to laugh at me because I'm friends with a girl. They call me horrible names and they've blocked me on our social media group so I can't chat with them. I feel very angry and unhappy, but I don't want to lose any of my friends. Please help me. What should I do?

6 What's the problem with RockStar's old friend?
7 Why does he feel angry and unhappy?

2 Talk to your partner about RockStar's post. Imagine that you are HeretoHelp.

1 Who can RockStar talk to?
2 What should he do?

3 Write a reply to RockStar's post. Use the words in the box.

might	should / shouldn't
need to	must / mustn't

Grammar reference

1 Going to

We use *going to* to talk about plans.

Affirmative	Negative	Question
I'm going to ride a bike.	I'm not going to ride a bike.	Am I going to ride a bike?
She's going to ride a bike.	She isn't going to ride a bike.	Is she going to ride a bike?
They're going to ride a bike.	They aren't going to ride a bike.	Are they going to ride a bike?

2 Will

We use *will* to talk about the future.

Affirmative	Negative	Question
It'll travel to the moon.	It won't travel to the moon.	Will it travel to the moon?
We'll travel to the moon.	We won't travel to the moon.	Will we travel to the moon?

3 Past continuous

We use the past continuous to describe what was happening in the past.

Affirmative	Negative	Question
I was working when you arrived.	I wasn't working when you arrived.	Was I working when you arrived?
He was working when you arrived.	He wasn't working when you arrived.	Was he working when you arrived?
They were working when you arrived.	They weren't working when you arrived.	Were they working when you arrived?

4 Countable and uncountable nouns

Countable nouns	Uncountable nouns
We can count them: apples, bananas, carrots	We can't count them: bread, sugar, water
How many bananas are there?	How much water is there?
There are too many bananas.	There's too much water.
There aren't many bananas.	There isn't much water.
There aren't enough bananas.	There isn't enough water.

5 Present perfect and adverbs

I still haven't done my homework. (= But I have to do it soon.)
She's been ill since Monday. (= When? A point in time: time, date, day, etc.)
They've been ill for two days. (= How long? How many minutes, hours, days, weeks, etc.)
Have you ever had a fish for a pet? (= At any time in your life)
I've never seen a dolphin. (= Not at any time in my life)

6 Pronouns

some someone something somewhere	any anyone anything anywhere	no no one nothing nowhere	every everyone everything everywhere

There's someone at the door.	There isn't anyone at the door. Is there anyone at the door?	There's no one at the door.	Everyone's at the door.
I've got something to tell you.	I haven't got anything to tell you. Have you got anything to tell me?	I've got nothing to tell you.	I'm going to tell you everything.
They're going somewhere.	They aren't going anywhere. Are they going anywhere?	They're going nowhere.	They're going everywhere.

7 Possibility

I may buy the skirt.
It might rain.
I may not buy the skirt.
It might not rain.

8 Present perfect and adverbs

You've just sent the email.	You haven't sent the email yet.	Have you sent the email yet?
She's already sent the email.	She hasn't sent the email yet.	Has she sent the email yet?

Flyers Listening Part 2

1 72 **Listen and complete the information. Then check with a partner.**

How do you spell that?

First name: Holly

1 Surname: ______

2 School: ______

3 Date of birth: 26th October ______

4 Library password: ______

5 I want to join because:

interested in ______

books can help with ______

2 73 **Listen and look. There is one example.**

A new adventure

Place opens for the first time:
on 3rd September

1 Visit to: ______ Castle

2 Age: ______ years old

3 Travel from village: by ______

4 Views of: ______

5 People like: the ______

Flyers Listening Part 3

1 74 **Listen. Write who the objects belong to. Use the box to help you. Then listen again and colour.**

Betty   Grace   ~~Oliver~~   Peter   Robert

2 75 **What did family and friends give George for his journey? Listen and write a letter in each box. There is one example.**

parents   best friend   geography teacher   grandma   cousin   uncle

a

b

c

d

e
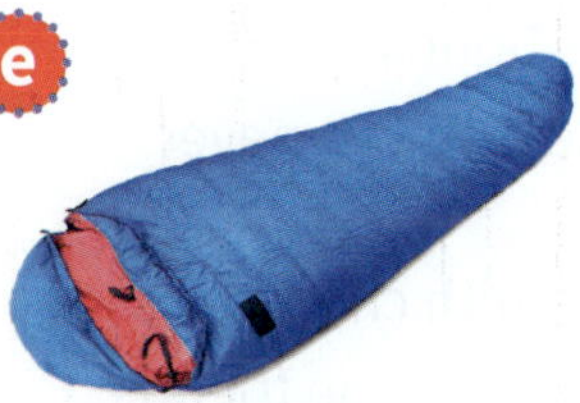

f

g

h

Flyers Reading and Writing Part 2

1 Read the sentences and choose the best answer. Draw lines and match. Then complete each answer in your notebook.

1 Shall we have a picnic in the park tomorrow afternoon?
2 The school bus might not come today because it's snowing!
3 Why is your grandma laughing?
4 What time will the train come?
5 Should I buy George a drum for his birthday?
6 Are you going to the concert tomorrow night?

A Oh, she's happy because…
B I think it arrives at…
C Good idea! I'll bring some popcorn and…
D No, he doesn't like…
E Yes, I'm really excited! It starts at…
F Oh no! We're going to be…

2 It's Monday afternoon. Richard is talking to Sophia about her birthday on Saturday. What does Sophia say? Read the text and choose the best answer. Write a letter (A–H) for each answer. You do not need to use all the letters. There is one example.

Example

Richard: Hi Sophia. What did you do for your birthday on Saturday?

Sophia: G

Questions

1 **Richard:** Where did you go?
Sophia: ______

2 **Richard:** Is that the one on the top floor of that new skyscraper?
Sophia: ______

3 **Richard:** Was the food good?
Sophia: ______

4 **Richard:** I hope you had a birthday cake!
Sophia: ______

5 **Richard:** Did you also go to the festival in the park that night?
Sophia: ______

A We went there after the meal. The music was brilliant.
B Of course! We all enjoyed a piece at home earlier.
C It was a new place called High Five.
D They're my favourite band.
E Yes! I ate a vegetable dish I've never tried before.
F It wasn't easy eating with chopsticks.
G My parents took me and some friends out to eat.
H Yes, the views were amazing!

Flyers Reading and Writing Part 4

1 Read and write the correct word.

1 Elephants ~~is~~ amazing animals.
_____are_____

2 Eating fruit and vegetables ~~all~~ day is healthy.
____

3 Skyscrapers are taller ~~that~~ trees.
____

4 Ponds are places ~~who~~ you find frogs.
____

5 One day people will ~~living~~ on the moon.
____

6 In the past, people ~~make~~ fires to cook on.
____

2 Read the text. Choose the right words and write them on the lines.

The tent

Example People _____have_____ used tents in different environments for thousands of years.

1 In the past, people lived in __________ because they didn't
2 have houses like we have today. People __________ stay in one place for very long. They took their animals to better places to feed in spring or winter and often walked
3 hundreds of kilometres __________ sell and buy food or important objects. Tents were heavy to carry but easy to make from trees and animal fur. They helped people feel safer at night.

4 __________, donkeys and camels carried explorers' tents on their long journeys
5 __________ jungles and across deserts to new countries. Tents also kept maps and diaries dry and safe.

6 Today, __________ is a popular activity for many families and friends at weekends
7 and holiday time. People enjoy __________ outside in a tent and being in the
8 countryside __________ from noisy, busy cities.

9 Tents are still usually the same shape __________ in the past but they are now made of lighter materials. Many people who love walking a lot on holiday can carry them
10 in or under their rucksacks. They are also easier to put up __________.

Example	did	can	(have)				
1	it	them	their	6	camp	camping	camped
2	don't	haven't	didn't	7	sleep	slept	sleeping
3	to	for	by	8	away	instead	over
4	Early	Next	Later	9	with	to	as
5	until	through	during	10	quick	quickly	quickest

Flyers Reading and Writing Part 6

1 Cross out the word that doesn't belong.

1 have … **time / fun / ~~hungry~~ / a headache**
2 go to … **bed / asleep / a hospital / school**
3 make … **friends / a cake / a noise / the doctor's**
4 be … **Spain / careful / tired / late**
5 take … **medicine / east / an exam / a bus**
6 feel … **well / cold / online / excited**

2 Read the diary and write the missing words. Write one word on each line.

Example	My dad ___has___ just started a new job and we've moved to a new city. I really love our new
1	apartment. It's on the 20th ____________, so the views are amazing.
2	Right now, my parents ____________ driving me to my new school.
3	I ____________ them I was feeling worried about my first day.
	Then Mum showed me there were four science lessons a week on the timetable. That made me happy
4	____________ it's my favourite subject!
5	There will ____________ a school skiing trip in winter, which sounds exciting too.
	I just hope my classmates are friendly!

Flyers Reading and Writing Part 7

1 **Look and write four or five words under each picture. Discuss your ideas with a partner. Then write a sentence for each picture in your notebook.**

2 **Look at the three pictures. Write about this story. Write 20 or more words.**

Flyers Speaking Part 3

1 Look and circle the words. Number the pictures in order.
Tell the story with your partner.

A scary cave

bicycle
blanket
creature
cave
river
castle
rucksack
rock

wood
desert
entrance
fire
beetle

gate
torch
pocket
sandwich
bat

2 These pictures tell a story. It's called 'Lucky Teddy'.
Just look at the pictures first. Now you tell the story.

Lucky Teddy!

Holly and her brother, David, are walking along a path next to a river with their mum and their dog. David wants to look at the waterfall.

Flyers Speaking Part 4

1 **Read the instructions. Play the game. Interview your partner.**

Instructions: Roll the dice only once each turn.
Go to the section on the game.
Answer your partner's questions.
Use the colour key to colour the Tell me square.
The winner is the first to answer all the questions and colour all the Tell me squares.

Tell me about your living room.

What do you do in the evenings after school?
What time do you get up on Sunday?
What are your favourite hobbies?

Tell me about a sport you like to do.

When is your birthday?
What do you like to eat on your birthday?
Where do you like to go?

Tell me about a special birthday present you've had.

Which places do you like going to in your town?
Where can you do sport?
What can you do in the park?

Tell me about your favourite shop.

What's your favourite time of year?
What did you do last summer?
How do you like to travel?

Tell me about things you like to do on holiday.

Where do you go to school?
How do you go to school?
What's your favourite subject?

Tell me about your school.

Do you live in a house or an apartment?
How many rooms are there?
Who lives with you?

Key:

green pink red blue orange purple

2 **Now listen and answer your teacher's questions.**

Thanks and Acknowledgements

Authors' thanks

Many thanks to everyone at Cambridge University Press and Assessment for their dedication and hard work, and in particular to:

Louise Wood for doing such a great job overseeing the level; Liz Wilkie for her hard work and great editorial assistance; freelance editors Melissa Bryant and Stephanie Howard.

We would also like to thank all our pupils and colleagues, past, present and future, at Star English academy in Murcia, especially Jim Kelly for his friendship and support throughout the years.

Dedications

For Alison Sharpe for seeing the potential, for Maria Pylas for driving it forward, for Susan Gonzalez for believing in and championing it, and for Liane Grainger for keeping us excellent, steadfast company throughout the whole of our stellar journey. – CN and MT

Illustration

Ana Sebastian (Bright Agency); Dave Williams (Bright Agency); David Belmont (Beehive); Javier Joaquin (Beehive); Laszlo Veres (Beehive); Moreno Chiacchiera (Beehive); Shahab (Sylvie Poggio Artists).

Audio

Audio production by Sounds Like Mike Ltd.

Video

Video acknowledgements are in the Teacher Resources on Cambridge One.

Design and typeset

Blooberry Design

Additional authors

Rebecca Legros (CLIL); Montse Watkin, (Sounds and Life Skills, Exam folder)

The authors and publishers acknowledge the following sources of copyright material and are grateful for the permissions granted. While every effort has been made, it has not always been possible to identify the sources of all the material used, or to trace all copyright holders. If any omissions are brought to our notice, we will be happy to include the appropriate acknowledgments on reprinting and in the next update to the digital edition, as applicable.

Key: U = Unit, R = Review, V = Values, EF = Exam folder

Photography

All photos are sourced from Getty Images.
U0: daboost/iStock/Getty Images Plus; Anastassiya Bezhekeneva/Moment; T3 Magazine/Future; JGI/Tom Grill/Tetra images; Daviles/iStock/Getty Images Plus; Lane Oatey/Blue Jean Images; kate_sept2004/E+; PonyWang/E+; Roman Bykhalets/iStock/Getty Images Plus; Lesia_G/iStock/Getty Images Plus; watchara_tongnoi/iStock/Getty Images Plus; Sergio Delle Vedove/EyeEm; SMSka/iStock/Getty Images Plus; Ilyabolotov/iStock/Getty Images Plus; **U1:** Klaus Vedfelt/DigitalVision; Neurobite/iStock/Getty Images Plus; MistikaS/E+; Keren Su/Photodisc; Helmut Meyer zur Capellen/imageBROKER; PHAS/Universal Images Group; DEA/A. DE GREGORIO/De Agostini; Dallas and John Heaton/The Image Bank Unreleased; Will \u0026 Deni McIntyre/Corbis Documentary; Image Source/DigitalVision; Thomas Barwick/DigitalVision; Peter Dazeley/The Image Bank; TPopova/iStock/Getty Images Plus; fcw5/iStock/Getty Images Plus; General Photographic Agency/Hulton Archive; stevenallan/iStock Unreleased; WILLSIE/iStock Editorial; ly86/DigitalVision Vectors; Lidiia Moor/iStock/Getty Images Plus; Naddiya/iStock/Getty Images Plus; invincible_bulldog/iStock/Getty Images Plus; Elen11/iStock/Getty Images Plus; MsMoloko/iStock/Getty Images Plus; seamartini/iStock/Getty Images Plus **U2:** Pascal Le Segretain/Getty Images Entertainment; mladn61/E+; artisteer/iStock/Getty Images Plus; RedBarnStudio/E+; Serjio74/iStock/Getty Images Plus; Vladimiroquai/iStock/Getty Images Plus; Stockbyte; Jonathan Knowles/Stone; dima_zel/iStock/Getty Images Plus; Frank Rossoto Stocktrek/DigitalVision; RichVintage/E+; FatCamera/E+; dima_zel/iStock/Getty Images Plus; Stocktrek Images; Bloomberg Creative/Bloomberg Creative Photos; skynesher/E+; gorodenkoff/iStock/Getty Images Plus; Jonathan Kitchen/DigitalVision; Nitat Termmee/Moment; Digital Art/The Image Bank; Mlenny/E+; egal/iStock/Getty Images Plus; Westend61; katatonia82/iStock/Getty Images Plus; vitalik19111992/iStock/Getty Images Plus; **U3:** Nastasic/DigitalVision Vectors; Dea Picture Library/De Agostini; Kurt Desplenter/AFP; Felix Cesare/Moment; Alexander Blotnitsky/AFP; Paul Souders/DigitalVision; evemilla/E+; Ryan McVay/Photodisc; herreid/iStock/Getty Images Plus; Engdao Wichitpunya/EyeEm; 4x6/E+; FangXiaNuo/E+; Christoph Wagner/Moment; VectorMine/iStock/Getty Images Plus; gniedzieska/iStock/Getty Images Plus; Â© Marco Bottigelli/Moment; Andre Schoenherr/Stone; Mark Garlick/Science Photo Library; -/AFP; **U4:** Aleksandr Zubkov/Moment; Burcu Atalay Tankut/Moment; FatManPhotoUK/iStock/Getty Images Plus; udra/iStock/Getty Images Plus; pilipphoto/iStock/Getty Images Plus; Roberto Machado Noa/Moment; Nirad/iStock/Getty Images Plus; Image Source; Natalya Trofimchuk/iStock/Getty Images Plus; fcafotodigital/E+; Carlo A/Moment; Milena_Vuckovic/iStock/Getty Images Plus; GMVozd/E+; Westend61; jointstar/iStock/Getty Images Plus; VvoeVale/iStock/Getty Images Plus; nehopelon/iStock/Getty Images Plus; The Washington Post; MaskaRad/iStock/Getty Images Plus; Anna Reinert/imageBroker; alvarez/E+; Steve Cicero/Photodisc; olgakr/iStock/Getty Images Plus; SiberianArt/iStock/Getty Images Plus; akkachai thothubthai/iStock/Getty Images Plus; sangidan idan/iStock/Getty Images Plus; **U5:** Ana Guisado Photography/Moment; Mike Hill/Stone; Catherine Falls Commercial/Moment; Hugh Threlfall/Moment Mobile; Gabriele Grassl/iStock/Getty Images Plus; nomadimagesuk/iStock/Getty Images Plus; Westend61; Robbie Goodall/Moment; C'est les photos que j'aime…/Moment; SolStock/E+; LeManna/iStock/Getty Images Plus; Burazin/The Image Bank; Andrea Gambadoro – Filmmaker and Photographer/Moment; Oleksandr Vakulin/EyeEm; Nattapong Leardprasit/EyeEm; George Karbus Photography/Image Source; Raimundo Fernandez Diez/Moment; Hal Beral/Corbis; by wildestanimal/Moment; Portra/DigitalVision; Ron Levine/DigitalVision; tetmc/iStock/Getty Images Plus; Tom Werner/DigitalVision; Jose Luis Pelaez Inc/DigitalVision; Humberto Ramirez/Moment; Andrew Peacock/Stone; VivianG/iStock/Getty Images Plus; Gabrielle Yap/EyeEm; Reinhard Dirscherl/The Image Bank; Ippei Naoi/Moment; Rajni Singh/EyeEm; Photo taken by Kami (Kuo, Jia-Wei)/Moment; alexander uhrin/iStock/Getty Images Plus; Vijay Talla/EyeEm; Silvia Otte/Stone; Puripatl/iStock/Getty Images Plus; Jeff J Mitchell/Getty Images News; eugenesergeev/iStock/Getty Images Plus; MrJub/iStock/Getty Images Plus; FoxysGraphic/iStock/Getty Images Plus; LuisAlvarez/Digital Vision **U6:** Purdue9394/E+; mediaphotos/iStock/Getty Images Plus; CasarsaGuru/E+; Robert Niedring/Cavan; Tgordievskaya/iStock/Getty Images Plus; Jupiterimages/Goodshoot; Westend61; Joe McBride/The Image Bank; lovro77/E+; FamVeld/iStock/Getty Images Plus; shironosov/iStock/Getty Images Plus; Seamind Panadda/EyeEm; brebca/iStock/Getty Images Plus; Wirote Banhachai/EyeEm; artproem/iStock/Getty Images Plus; DougLemke/iStock/Getty Images Plus; Aneese/iStock/Getty Images Plus; soopareuk/iStock/Getty Images Plus; Nikada/iStock Unreleased; Monty Rakusen/Image Source; DigitalVision; FoxysGraphic/iStock/Getty Images Plus; prospero_design/E+ **U7:** Yobro10/iStock/Getty Images Plus; Antonio_Diaz/iStock/Getty Images Plus; Brian Mitchell/Corbis Documentary; damircudic/E+; Mario Marco/Moment; Weerayut Ranmai/EyeEm; Ng Sok Lian/EyeEm; Kwanchai Lerttanapunyaporn/EyeEm; MirageC/Moment; Alicia Llop/Moment; Image Source; Mali Li Lxm/EyeEm; Last Resort/Photodisc; popovaphoto/iStock/Getty Images Plus; Prasert Krainukul/Moment; olegbreslavtsev/iStock/Getty Images Plus; pearleye/E+; Andrei Naumenka/iStock/Getty Images Plus; SEAN GLADWELL/Moment; bubaone/DigitalVision Vectors; Maydaymayday/DigitalVision Vectors; smartboy10/DigitalVision Vectors; **U8:** SDI Productions/E+; kali9/E+; ferrantraite/E+; Pongasn68/iStock/Getty Images Plus; Razvan/iStock Editorial; Mekdet/Moment; lukyeee1976/iStock/Getty Images Plus; luchschen/iStock/Getty Images Plus; janrysavy/E+; Imgorthand/E+; Tom Werner/DigitalVision; monkeybusinessimages/iStock/Getty Images Plus; Paul Wigfield/EyeEm; Richmatts/E+; SHansche/iStock/Getty Images Plus; isil terzioglu/iStock/Getty Images Plus; Mark Astakhov/iStock/Getty Images Plus; AndyRoland/iStock/Getty Images Plus; Ennessy/iStock/Getty Images Plus; **R26:** narvikk/E+; **R44:** kali9/E+; **R62:** Jon Hicks/Stone; Jupiterimages/Photos.com\u003e; FG Trade/E+; Tetra Images; Yellow Dog Productions/The Image Bank; Marc Dufresne/E+; monkeybusinessimages/iStock/Getty Images Plus; Ariel Skelley/DigitalVision; **R80:** FG Trade/E+; Stocktrek Images; ratmaner/iStock/Getty Images Plus; Shedu/iStock/Getty Images Plus; ttatty/iStock/Getty Images Plus; Sebastian Ramirez Morales/Moment; leitmotif425/iStock/Getty Images Plus; 3djewelry/iStock/Getty Images Plus; wanderluster/E+; Carlos Salsamendi/EyeEm; blackCAT/E+; AleksandarNakic/E+; Ekaterina Pereslavtseva/EyeEm; Barry Austin/DigitalVision; Chris Tobin/DigitalVision; Noel Hendrickson/DigitalVision; Jamie Grill/Tetra images; Westend61; Sam Edwards/OJO Images; Jaakko Paarvala/Moment; Alistair Berg/DigitalVision; Caia Image/Collection Mix: Subjects; **V82:** ConceptCafe/iStock/Getty Images Plus; **V84:** JGI/Tom Grill/Tetra images; MoMo Productions/DigitalVision; **V85:** lushik/DigitalVision Vectors; Anna Erastova/iStock/Getty Images Plus; **EF:** Johner Images/Johner Images Royalty-Free; Westend61; Oliver Rossi/DigitalVision; David A Land/Tetra images; Tom Merton/OJO Images; eurobanks/iStock/Getty Images Plus; Tim Robberts/DigitalVision; vav63/iStock/Getty Images Plus; Amphawan Chanunpha/iStock/Getty Images Plus; benimage/E+; skodonnell/E+; lucentius/E+; phwphr bdinthr phathr/EyeEm; valio84sl/iStock/Getty Images Plus; barisonal/E+; Ganesh Bastola/Moment; Maskot; Inti St Clair/DigitalVision.

Cover photography by Tiffany Mumford for Creative Listening.

Commissioned photography by Stephen Noble and Duncan Yeldham for Creative Listening.